MW01182008

ANTIFREEZE COOKBOOK

The true story of murder and corruption in small town Arkansas

Tonya York

As told to

Chris Hancock

1

For David and all those who have suffered needless loss

Thanks to my mom and brother Billy

Advance Praise:

Tracy J. Horne, it's been a long journey, a journey I'm thankful you chose to take. I'm forever grateful to have been blessed to have your expertise, guidance, and advice. Without you, this book would not exist.

I would like to express my gratitude to Chris Hancock. Without his superb writing ability, my story could not have been told to its fullest.

I thank Professor Mark Spitzer, for his kind support, and the time he took out of his own busy schedule to edit the book and help with an amazing title.

All names have been changed to protect the innocent and deny notoriety to the guilty.

Preface/Synopsis

I walked out of her office with my suspicion affirmed, with the first hope of conclusion since my brother's unexplained death years earlier. This revelation gave me the confidence to persist in my search for answers.

Years of investigation would uncover falsified paperwork, nonstandard procedures, frightening ignorance of state law and many conspicuous coincidences. Dangerous negligence would range from a lazy doctor to an apathetic state prosecutor. A suspect would run across America while the heat died down, cooled by an accomplice in local law enforcement.

There were no reliable narrators so I found a voice. Today, justice is delayed by one missing piece. There is warmth, still, in this chilling account. More than a tragedy, this story offers hope that wounds can close.

"Justice denied anywhere diminishes justice everywhere" MLK JR

"Time is the justice that examines all offenders" Shakespeare

"The truth does not cease to exist because it's ignored" Aldous Huxley

Chapter 1

Our houses were near enough that we saw each other as I walked across the porch and my brother David drove toward the corner store. Something was different about him. His big brown eyes lacked their usual light. He didn't crack his signature sunrise smile, or give a big wave, or honk his truck's horn playfully. He gave a stiff, pained, nod that made me wish I could tell him he didn't have to be so polite, that I could tell he didn't feel good.

It was strange for him to be home from work this early on a Monday. David took his work very seriously. He was only twenty-eight and already a manufacturing supervisor. He was rarely absent. He was charged with meeting deadlines, regardless of which employees called in sick or had to be absent. Everyone knew that for David to miss work he had to be very sick or have had an emergency that justified all the catch up work he'd have to do when he returned. David had always felt he would be setting a bad example if he missed work for anything less. He never wanted to add any difficulty to another person's day. He was a problem solver, passing the buck to someone else was against his constitution.

It was always ominous to see David at home during his working hours. Something had to be very wrong.

It was warm enough to feel the sun's heat sinking into my skin, brisk enough that a breath of cool breeze could blow away the warmth of tawny sunlight. The wind was confused—a warm breeze this way, a cooler one crossing over, intermingling like a glass of fresh sweet tea, warm from brewing but poured over ice, warmth and chill, stirring like autumn air. Little leafy whirlwinds gathered themselves up from the curbs and spun themselves out in the street, exasperated, short-winded. In lulls between breezes it almost felt balmy until a sour-sweet gust crisped the air with the chilled citrus of fermenting foliage.

When I walked back inside the house, I asked Mom about him.

"He's sick," she said.

Knowing David, I knew this had to be an understatement. I feared he might have a virus. I wondered if he should even be driving, but I knew he could be stubborn. I wished he would have asked one of us to go get what he needed from the store. But that was David. He avoided asking for things, even when we asked him to make a request. Family members thought he was hard to shop for, but what he said was true, that he'd always be happy with everyone's company.

I hoped David would just get his crackers and Sprite and sleep this sickness away. I decided I should go check on him later. It had been a few days since I had seen him anyway, which was rare; I went to visit nearly every day.

But I did not go see him later, for whatever regrettable reason. I noticed all of the lights in his home were off. I checked periodically to see if he had woken up and turned on a light. I couldn't risk waking him up if he was resting. Later I got tangled in life's loose ends, the laundry of life, and found myself running errands and chasing half-tasks. As dusk fell that evening, I joined a friend to watch movies and I planned to see David tomorrow, hoping he would feel better.

It was September 19, 1994. It had been six years since our family moved to Perryville, Arkansas. My parents and I lived on B Street. My brother David and his wife Katrina lived on A Street.

My sister Sarah called David and Katrina's house at 8:30 that night. Katrina answered. Sarah asked if she could speak to David.

"Oh girl, he's sick. He's lying down and I'm sorry, but he can't come to the phone right now."

About two hours later, my father was speaking with our sister Kate, on his home phone. This was before the current ubiquity of cell phones had reached Perryville. My mother had just left the house for work in Conway. She was a quality control supervisor. She left the house at exactly 10:30 pm in order to be at work by 11:00 pm. We all knew this. She did this without fail, Monday through Friday. She was punctual and dependable. You could set your watch by her routine departures for work.

Mom had only been gone a few minutes when Dad's conversation with Kate was interrupted by another incoming call. It was his son's home number.

"Just a second, Kate, David's calling," he said and put her on hold.

But it wasn't my brother on the line. It was David's wife, my sister-in-law, Katrina; she was screaming, "Something's wrong with David! Get over here quick!" she repeated hysterically.

Dad got back on the line with Kate. "Got to go, something's wrong with David." He hung up before hearing any of her startled questions.

He chugged toward his vehicle, moving quickly despite the toll his recent heart surgery had taken on his body. He was supposed to be resting and recovering but when your child needs you, even if they're no longer a child, you find a way to get there. It's parent power. Dad still had his parent power even though he was a grandparent now.

Dad charged a block away to David and Katrina's house on A Street and burst in through the door, with no spare second for knocking. He found Katrina inside, staring at the door, waiting for him. She told him David was in the bedroom.

Dad found him gray and blue, cold to the touch—a stark contrast to his usual athletic vitality. He was motionless, seeming to shiver with stillness, the frozen hue and tremble of burn-blanched paper ash, a cold blue flame fighting for life.

Katrina followed Dad into the bedroom, repeating "PLEASE BE OKAY, PLEASE BE OKAY" monotonously, like a chant, an incantation, so that after a moment the repetitive sound swallowed itself and Dad didn't hear her anymore.

Waiting for the ambulance, Dad was overcome with a frantic anxiety. He assumed Katrina had already called one. He knew the EMT station was right next door, on the same property as the Sheriff's Department. Why weren't they here yet?

In this purgatory of terrible waiting, Dad tried to comfort his son, not really sure what to do, just squeezing and staring at David's face, squeezing and staring, trying to revive him, trying to warm him. Dad did the best he could to share his warmth with my brother.

Dad was red with nervous heat. This was exactly the degree of stress and exertion his doctor had forbidden. His shirt hung heavy, saturated with sweat, cheeks burning. The brimming puddles in his eyes were camouflaged by the boiling perspiration running over his brow, dripping down—sweat and tears mixing, spilling salt to the earth.

Katrina continued chanting "PLEASE BE OKAY, PLEASE BE OKAY" —a screaming meditation.

Dad's fear turned to fury, and he yelled out, cradling his unresponsive son, "WHERE'S THE AMBULANCE?"

It had already been several minutes since he had arrived. It should have come by now.

"Oh! I haven't!" Katrina squawked, crumbling into debilitated blubber.

"Oh my God! Oh my God!" she hollered again and again. She took no action to grab the phone off the wall and make the call.

Dad scrambled out of the bedroom, where he was holding David, in a fearful rage to find the phone.

A former EMT was at home next door and one of Katrina's friends, a medical professional, across the street knew CPR but she hadn't thought to seek help from either of them, or call for help. Professional help was all around her.

After Dad called the ambulance, he called our pastor. They were close friends. My Dad needed some counsel through this unfolding horror, a nightmare he had never dreamed. It had just begun.

Mom was getting anxious at work after trying to call Dad at home. He was supposed to be recuperating from his surgery. As another call went unanswered she tried to avoid leaping to worst-case scenarios.

My sister Kate soon arrived at David's house with her husband Thomas to see what was going on after hearing Dad's worrying words just before he had hung up on her. Shortly after they walked in to see David, the ambulance finally arrived.

Two EMTs rushed in. They didn't ask any questions beyond where David was. They hurried to put him on the gurney. They didn't speak; their silence worried my father even more.

David was tall and muscular. In this catatonic state he was extremely difficult to move. The EMTs fumbled him to the floor of the living room as they carried him out. You can imagine how difficult that was for the family to see.

My Dad knew he would have to go pickup Mom from work in Conway before going to the hospital, so he directed Katrina to ride with our pastor to the emergency room. Katrina agreed, but before walking out, she went to a back bedroom and called the children out, Lindsey, Madeline, and Sawyer. Dad had assumed the kids weren't home until then. He was surprised they hadn't come out to see what was happening. They had clearly been forbidden from leaving that room or surely all of this commotion would have drawn them out. Katrina sent the kids across the street to her friend's house—the one who knew CPR.

I was still at my friend's house when Mom called me to ask if I would run home and check on Dad. I hurried home to put Mom at ease but I expected to find Dad safely dozed off in his chair.

On the way over to my parent's house I saw ambulance lights flickering red and blue into the barren branches, illuminating the night near my brother's house. As I approached, I realized it was parked in front of David's house.

At first thought, I was worried for my Dad, afraid there had been some post-operation complication. Then I feared that one of the kids had been hurt. Splinters of dread flashed through my mind as I drove closer, but I hadn't entertained the possibility of David being hurt. He was too strong for my worry to leap to him immediately.

As I pulled up, the ambulance sped away. I saw my sister-in-law Katrina get in our pastor's car before it pulled out following the ambulance. I parked and ran into the house, pushing through the front door, which had been left ajar.

My stride was broken when I bumped into my brother-in-law Thomas as he was walking out. He was a big strong guy, in body and spirit. Thomas was not one to be rattled; his appearance filled me with instant dread—his eyes swollen wide open, his face washed-out white as this page and blank with shock.

"David didn't look good" was all he said to me before walking outside to get some air.

I pushed into the house where I found Dad and Kate in hand-wringing distress, trying to make a plan.

"What happened to David?" I asked.

They didn't hear me at first, in the midst of this chaos.

"We need to call Mom and tell her whatever is happening and that you're okay," I told my Dad.

"No, not yet," he told me. "Call but don't use your Mom's extension. Leave a message at the front desk that I am fine and we are on our way to pick her up. We can't have her worrying by herself while she waits on us. We'll explain on the ride back to the hospital."

I still didn't know what had happened. I tried to put this shattered puzzle together but too many pieces were still missing. The urgency to find answers, and fear of what they might be, prevented me from assembling any more coherent questions.

We left a hurried message for Mom and filed out to Dad's car. As we loaded up, one of David and Katrina's neighbors approached us like he had been waiting for us to step out of the house. He asked my Dad what had happened. This man had previously worked as an EMT and had seen the ambulance pull away a couple of minutes before.

"Something happened to David. We don't know yet. We're going to get his mother and we're headed to the hospital. We have to go."

This neighbor expressed his regret that he hadn't known earlier. He might have helped. He wished someone had grabbed him.

As my Dad turned to get behind the wheel, the neighbor said something that caused Dad to pause in his rush.

"Cain was there earlier. Thought that was strange. I saw him leave around eight o'clock."

There was a rumor that Katrina had been having an affair with Cain. We had all heard it, but we never talked about it. Cain worked in the Perry County Sheriff's Office. He was about twenty years older than Katrina. I had never heard of a thirty-two-year-old wife cheating on her twenty-eight-year-old husband with a man old enough to be her father.

"...that is strange, thanks" Dad said as he got in the car and we hurdled out of Perryville to get Mom in Conway.

There were no answers yet, only questions, so many questions that we were tongue-tied in silence for a moment. There were too many things to say to choose one thing to say first.

It felt as though we were driving in the wrong direction. David, in that ambulance, headed to St. Vincent Hospital in Morrilton, us headed on to Conway. We had to drive away from him in order to come back and be with him. We had to go so we could get back.

Kate began asking questions. "What happened, is he sick? What did Katrina say?"

Dad seemed to be a world apart from us, leaning as he drove with his temple against the window. His only response; "She did it. She finally did it."

The drive passed in slow-motion then jarred forward in flashes. The daily rhythm of passing minutes collapsed into this discordant and surreal nightmare time.

When we arrived at Mom's workplace in Conway, our car hadn't fully stopped before Mom was in the passenger seat. She was already in a worried fever despite Dad not telling her about David over the phone. I saw it in her eyes; she already felt something was terribly wrong. She seemed to already know, except for the details. She was hyper-aware, heightened by that instinct that haunts mothers. Still, I saw a fleeting relief in her eyes after she saw Dad was driving.

He was okay, after all. But that alleviation was instantly replaced by the anxiety of wondering what had caused her post-op husband and two of her daughters to come retrieve her from work when her shift had just begun

Her frantic motherly interrogation began as Dad drove to get back on the interstate.

"What's happened?"

"David", Dad tried to tell her.

Mom proceeded to ask all the questions my sister and I had thought to ask and more. We listened in, hoping to hear a shred of explanation. But Dad only expressed his confusion and anger. My sister and I looked at each other, now realizing why Dad hadn't told us anything. He didn't know either.

All he could tell us was how he found David, how he tried to warm him up, how mad he was that Katrina hadn't thought to call the ambulance immediately, and what the neighbor had said about Cain. He described a brown fluid coming out of David's nose and mouth. The wretched smell had challenged everyone to reign in their gag reflexes.

The drive to the hospital was dappled with fidgeting silences. We were all leaning forward in our seats to get there even a second sooner, muscles twitching from being unconsciously flexed, suspended in suspense.

We alternately speculated in a fervor, all of us thinking about how much we did not know—question marks in our restless blustery eyes, tremors in our voices.

Finally, we pulled up to the hospital in Morrilton, a building I had passed a million times before but was now newly ominous and forbidding with its moth-fluttered lights projecting overlapping shadows. Red and yellow lights numbly hummed without warmth. "EMERGENCY" glowed too calmly to communicate what that word means.

As Dad pulled into the circle by the E.R. doors, we saw Katrina sitting on the bricks surrounding a hospital sign. The cherry of her cigarette glowed, a lone red eye, before she flicked it away. I told Dad to stop and I hopped out and ran toward her to ask what had happened. Surely she would know. She was the only one who had been with David the whole time. She would have some answers.

Katrina sat there, stoic and tearless. She hadn't forgotten to bring her cigarettes. This reassured me. Her disaffected demeanor gave me a small sense of relief. If she was taking a smoke break, the situation could be fixed.

When I reached her I asked with half a breath, "What's going on?"

She instantly burst into tears; from stone-faced to streaming in a split-second. Dread flooded back into me, lifting a buoyant lump into my throat. Katrina wasn't usually one to concede any vulnerability.

Then she said something between wails that made me dizzy, that drained everything of color. My vision flattened as a dimension of my world deflated.

"David is gone."

Until that point I had not entertained the possibility of losing my brother that night. Those three words knocked the wind out of me. This was all real. This was happening. I caught my breath.

"But I didn't even get to see him," I protested, as if I had found an unraveling flaw in her assessment, a reason he couldn't be gone.

A sharp shard of laughter escaped from her. It was all the more distinct for her fruitless effort to contain it—like the squeaking snicker of children in church trying to pinch their mouths closed. An elastic smirk peeled over her teeth. She struggled to hold herself—like a child questioned about a prank, trying to hide some pride in it.

It was warm that night, but a chill crept up my neck. I took a step back, then another. She processed my stricken face and just as quickly as that snicker had escaped from her, she clapped her mouth shut and darted her eyes to the ground.

In that same second, my mother began screaming at the E.R. doors. My brother Robert had just told Mom that her exuberant, healthy, twenty-eight-year-old son was pronounced dead on arrival. After hearing that heart-wrenching cry, that beacon of chaos from my mother, a pillar of strength and guidance, I could no longer deny the terrible reality closing in around us. My brother was surely gone. I left Katrina at the sign and ran toward my mother as she shouted at our pastor "Where's your God now? WHERE?"

Dr. Mallard was on call that night. Everyone in town knew that he was sort of a quack, not actively malicious but careless. As many of life's complications result from such quiet mediocrity as violent aggression, red in tooth and nail. It was common for people to reschedule with another doctor after being assigned an appointment with him, even when it meant a longer waiting period or driving out of town. Dr. Mallard was late in his career at this small town hospital and he was not inclined to stay abreast in his profession. He was known to be biding his time, slouching toward retirement. His expertise had obsolesced, his Hippocratic Oath expired.

The doctor and two nurses had worked on David for a few minutes and quickly pronounced him D.O.A. Cause of death: Myocardial Infarction; otherwise known as a heart attack. This sloppy diagnosis was employed as an ambiguous catchall. Of course a man's heart stops when he passes. There was no certain cause of death. David's arrested heart was a symptom, not a cause.

They had already rolled him out of the E.R. into a side room. I walked inside through the double glass doors of the E.R. entrance. I squinted as the bleary-bright fluorescent light washed over me. I breathed in the sterile powdery smell of hospitals everywhere. The walls, the floor, the scrubs, everything, was a watery pastel blue dissolving into monotonous gray.

I remembered the last time our family was all gathered in a hospital. We were in Little Rock after

Dad's heart attack. We all sat in the waiting room, waiting to hear about Dad and waiting for David to arrive. Impatient for him to get there, I walked to the parking lot to wait for him. When I got to the doors I saw him walking in the automatic doors, carrying a woman. He delivered her to a chair and went to the intake desk and spoke with a nurse.

He told me the woman had been in the parking lot waiting for someone to help her into the hospital. She had a broken leg and could not walk.

We stayed at the hospital late into the night. After hearing that Dad was stable and resting, we all decided to go eat. It was two or three in the morning and none of us had eaten dinner. Because it was so late, our options for restaurants were limited. We stopped at a twenty-four-hour diner franchise.

About the time our waitress brought our orders to the table, two men walked by and I saw David's face change. He watched them walk to their seats.

"We're leaving. Everyone get up," he said.

We were confused by this, of course. We stalled and looked at each other.

"Get up, we're leaving," he said again, already standing.

We all got up and walked toward the door. He followed us out, after informing the manager of the situation, all the while keeping an eye on that table where the men had sat.

"Those guys had guns," David explained as we pulled out. He had seen a bulge in the back of one of their waists and on the other man a gun was clearly visible, tucked into the back of his pants.

The next day we saw on the news that there had been a shooting at that same restaurant less than an hour after we had left.

David was a leader and protector. He was an observer. He carried people. He was a rescuer, and now I wondered how we could rescue our rescuer.

As I struggled to orient myself walking around in circles of identical hospital hallways, a lady behind a counter said, "David?" I nodded and was led into the room where they had put him. I wasn't prepared for what I saw when I came around the corner. He looked scarier than anyone with stage makeup I had seen in the movies. I jumped, and grew more upset, feeling guilty for being scared by his appearance. The staff had left the door open. Anyone could've walked in, or been easily startled passing by this room. This was disrespectful.

I could already see the blood settled, pulled down by gravity, pooled toward his posterior. I could see a line clear enough to follow with a marker, horizontally along his arms, abdomen, legs. He looked half empty. Dad, Kate and Thomas confirmed he had looked as moldered as this even at the house just before the ambulance arrived.

Later, our pastor shared that David's appearance had disturbed him as well. He had counseled many grieving individuals and families throughout his career of ministry. He had been called on many grungy nights like this one. He had spent a lot of empathetic hours at hospitals, but he had never seen anyone look like David had that night.

Why did they have to wheel him out and discard him so quickly? The E.R. was not particularly busy. It certainly was not overflowing. We were the only family there at the time.

I never even saw Dr. Mallard myself; he had already gone. Maybe he wanted the E.R. empty so his shift could end.

Standing there, staring at David, I had an urge to cut his hair. I looked around for scissors. Maybe the hair could be tested to figure out what had happened. There were no scissors to be found.

That night my mother signed the papers to have an autopsy performed, but we didn't know at the time that it didn't matter because, legally, Katrina was next-of-kin so an autopsy required her consent. We didn't expect getting her approval would be a problem.

When a family member passes at the hospital it is common practice that they contact the family's preferred funeral home. The funeral director arrived shortly before my parent's sought Katrina's consent to allow an autopsy. He soon joined my parents in arguing with Katrina for an hour, at least, trying to convince her to allow it.

My Mom tried to reason with her. "Katrina, this could be some sort of hereditary thing. I have other children and grandchildren. You have children that might be affected. We need to know. What if Madeline or Sawyer have inherited a ticking time bomb?"

Katrina finally gave in, but she was irate. I can see her anger in her signature from that night—a wild scrawl scarred into the paper. Was this not a painful mystery to her as well? We were all vexed by her adamant resistance to discovering exactly why David was gone. Surprise was extinct to me now. I expected the worst.

There is no reason a healthy and athletic twenty-eight-year-old, with no history of medical complications, should pass so suddenly of unexplained causes and not have an autopsy. Besides the common sense of it, we later discovered that it is also Arkansas State Law.

Statute 12-12-315 guarantees David an autopsy for a variety of reasons, including: (A) Homicide, suicide, and accidental death could not be ruled out (B) His death could have been the result of drugs or poisons in the body (L) His manner of death appeared to be other than natural (M) The death was sudden and unexplained, and (R) The death likely occurred in the home (David was pronounced D.O.A. at the hospital. The two paramedics one being the deputy coroner at the time, later told my parents that they knew it was too late as soon as they saw David.)

Katrina stood there with her arms locked across her chest, impervious, with wavy shoulder-length blonde hair, in pink shorts and a white shirt. Her flip-flops smacked as she began pacing. Her always perfectly manicured natural nails, were unsurprisingly perfect even in the tumult of this night. Her only rebuttal of my parent's heartbroken request, which she repeated in her repetitive style, was that she "just wanted it all to be over."

But for the rest of us this wouldn't be over until we knew why he was gone. Evidently, she wanted this "over" at the expense of any explanation or conclusion. Her argument was nonsensical. But at least she finally signed for the autopsy, angry as she was. We had to know why.

I can still remember the weather perfectly that night, September 19, 1994. When I sit and close my eyes I can feel the warm air breathing over my skin. It was warm, not hot, cool, not cold. A mild breeze stirred languidly. Fog lingered here and there in depressions of the landscape which I found overly appropriate, as if a fog machine had been brought in to make this nightmare more surreal.

The hardest part was seeing David rolled out of the hospital on a gurney, completely covered up and belted down and placed in the waiting white hearse. I stood, numb, watching it all. I had to resist the urge to run over and jerk the cover off of David's head so he could breathe.

Then I wanted to stop the funeral director from taking him... I just wanted to take David home. I kept thinking *He'll be okay if we can just get him home.* My next thought, watching his body being loaded, was, *I need to take him back inside so another doctor can try to help him one more time, just to be sure.*

After he was loaded, the door slammed shut under its own weight...I can still hear it—such an open-ended closing. It echoes in memory.

My eyes never left the white hearse as it drove away. It travelled beyond my sight, evaporating into the gauzy night and the fog of sunken clouds.

I had never been more crushed, more vulnerable, more confused, but I wasn't crying, which can only be explained as a symptom of my utter shock. I held on to the rationalization that this was just some sort of test, that if I cried I might make it real, that my conceded tears might authorize this nightmare as reality. For a moment, I tried not to acknowledge it for fear of making it true. But like a flimsy dam trying to retain an ocean, I inevitably broke down. Sour briny tears rolled with more gravity than I could contain.

I remember saying his name, *"David,"* in a whisper. That was not David I had seen loaded into the white hearse. It was just his body. David was gone.

I stood there a while in the E.R. parking lot, sinking into the ground, anchored in place in a stripe of moonlight, unnaturally fluorescent. The damp smell of magnolia in early fall replaced the hospital's stale air in my lungs. It is the most devastated I have ever been.

What do you do after watching that? There is no obvious next step. This was a rupture in reality. This was an inconclusive segue to nothing. This moment was islanded from the greater fabric of passing time, an isolated patch only the size of the feet on which I stood, a dot surrounded by vast void.

My brother Robert was kneeling beside the hospital, never one to express emotion, yet weeping, hushed, for his stolen brother. The stars in the sky were oddly bright. There were no city lights dimming the glitter above me. The stars melted and blurred and burst into one another through the tear-damp lenses of my eyes.

I asked God to please take care of David.

Chapter 2

The following day my parents called the funeral home to ask if their son's body had been returned from the State Crime Lab in Little Rock where the autopsy was to be performed. They were informed that his body had never been taken to the Medical Examiner.

Katrina had called the State Crime Lab in that short window of time elapsed since the previous evening and, as legal next-of-kin, she cancelled the autopsy that our family had agreed on at the hospital.

Today, I wonder how the State Crime Lab was manipulated or how the facts were misrepresented to obfuscate the unknowns surrounding David's death. I wonder what convoluted communication occurred to allow this gross ignorance of State Law. An autopsy was not a choice to make; it was required by law given the circumstances. David's mysterious and sudden death satisfied multiple requirements for an autopsy. Somehow, Katrina's preference trumped the enforcement of State Law, whether calculated or negligent.

Dr. Mallard has since passed, but my mother has received written statements from the two nurses on duty that night, both stating their belief that an autopsy should have been requested because of the oddity of David's death. They told us afterward that they could tell as soon as David was wheeled in that something was unusual about his condition. His discoloration and the rapid onset of rigor mortis were not typical of someone so recently deceased. According to them, a drive from Perryville to Morrilton would not have taken long enough for David to have progressed to that stage.

By the time we found out that the autopsy had been sabotaged, my parents felt too much time had already passed since David's death. They were understandably stressed, depressed and shocked. This turmoil drained them of the energy it would take to legally contest the cancelled autopsy and still allow for a timely burial. Katrina's bullying wore them down. It was an emotional battle of attrition. Katrina succeeded in making them feel silly for delaying their son's preparation and burial by accusing them of being selfish in their insistence on an autopsy.

My parents were afraid that Katrina did have control of this situation because the crime lab had accepted her cancellation over their request. They conceded to move forward with the funeral, having to painfully accept they might never know what took their son.

Mom and Dad were broken and exhausted and Katrina, always playing her game, exploited the opportunity to rush things along. She just wanted it to "all be over," as she kept reminding us. She eroded the will of my parents like water cracks foundations, pooling in low spots and looking for cracks—freezing, melting, then freezing again, disarming warmth followed by sharp ice, wedging open the slightest weakness.

The only available supplement for a true conclusion was laying my brother to rest. Katrina met us at the funeral home when we went to select a casket.

At one point, the salesman pulled out a white casket. This wasn't the first or last casket we looked at. It was immediately clear that my mother preferred that casket. As soon as it was displayed, she looked to my Dad with her eyes of approval.

Katrina had yet to shed a tear throughout this trauma but suddenly she broke down. She had only one gear to cry in, all or nothing, on or off. Her mood could turn like a page in a book; from smug to hysterical, icy to melting tears. She could be seething over the slightest non-issue then turn around sweet enough to make your teeth hurt.

"Pick whichever you want," Katrina said and left. She took no further role in the arrangements. At the time I was surprised and temporarily comforted to see her act human—as if reality had finally hit her. I considered if the reason she had been so collected awaiting her insurance collection was because she was in some grave denial. But then again, maybe these were canned crocodile tears, easy as turning on a faucet. Maybe this break down was a diversion, a license to leave. Maybe she had some other errand to run, maybe with Cain.

I wondered if Katrina's reaction would influence my mother's decision. It didn't. It was obvious that the white casket was Mom's choice before Katrina coughed tears and exited. My mother ultimately decided that she preferred it so it was chosen.

I feared Katrina would bring up this benign choice at the funeral and make a scene, accuse my parents of trying to spite her. I considered warning my parents. But the thought of letting Katrina's machinations influence our family's decision seemed immediately ridiculous. She had no desire to participate.

As you might expect, after the autopsy refusal, relations were chilly between Mom and Katrina. But my mother is friendly to a fault and their interactions were measured but civil.

Maybe Katrina had finally faced reality when she saw that particular casket. Maybe she realized Mom liked it and she felt the need to make a statement against it—another game to win. To Katrina, life is a contest first and foremost. She is always keeping score. In the absence of an overt competition, Katrina will engineer a score to keep, sometimes even competing to be the more pitiable victim, competing for sympathy. If anyone has had a bad day, her day has been worse. After hearing anyone's sad story, she has a more tragic one.

Katrina always has a story to tell. The scenario is always grandiose. The more her unsuspecting audience shows polite interest the more fantastic the story becomes. She one-ups herself, contradicting her own tales as her performance escalates. She juices her audience of empathy and awe. The fact that the world is out to get her supplies limitless material.

During family night she shed no tears. She was quite talkative, even laughing at times. She crafted textbook chit-chat, chiming in scripted clichés of mourning. "He's in a better place," "I'll always have him in my heart." She inserted Hallmark phrases without emotion.

Katrina had forgotten it was this white casket that had caused her breakdown. But I remembered. It was strange to me that she made no mention of it. The very fact that she neglected such an opportunity for dramatic conflict signaled that she did not remember. She didn't make the connection. These were just peripheral details for her.

The majority of our extended family was present for family night on the evening before the funeral. Everyone was in quiet shock at her apparent lack of feeling. Relatives and family friends milled around, consoling and catching up with each other the way families do in such circumstances.

I was newly aware of gravity. It had become heavier. I walked on bruised leaden heels. The spotless high-pile carpet felt like heavy mud. The adage that "time heals all" was useless now that time refused to pass. Wandering among relatives, I drudged along under this new weight, afraid to be still for fear of sinking.

Katrina stared straight through us, as if this crisis was all in our heads, just some psychosomatic rash sure to clear up if we only followed her example and ignored it. Her hard smile looked like it hurt. She sat talking and pretending to listen, feigning interest, nodding to keep people chattering. She excelled at getting people to talk about themselves, to self-disclose as she absently tapped her long manicured nails together making a hollow clicking sound and rubbing her fingers over her nail tips, always perfect.

After a while, I realized I hadn't seen Sawyer, David and Katrina's six-year-old son. Theresa, David's ex-wife, and I began asking around and looking for him in different rooms, growing increasingly worried the longer our search drug on. We finally found him crouched under a stack of chairs in a darkened side room. He was alone, scared and confused.

We coaxed Sawyer out of this cave he had retreated to and spoke with him about what was going on—like his mother should have done. He was so young, so new to life and unaware of death. He had no idea what was happening. We soon discovered Katrina hadn't told him anything. He was left completely in the dark and had sought out this storage room to hide from the tumult.

I could hear Katrina in the next room making conversation, laughing, disaffected.

After we calmed Sawyer down and answered some simple questions about where his Daddy had gone, the three of us mixed back into the clusters of conversing relatives. Some of them reflected aloud, some simply stood quietly together.

After Theresa's show of strength, trying her best to comfort Sawyer, tears began escaping her despite her visible effort to retain the wells in her eyes. She wanted to go into the chapel and spend a few minutes with David, but she was nervous about the possibility of Katrina finding her in there. I told her not to worry, just to go. She only had tonight for last words.

But Theresa was still worried about Katrina. My sister Sarah walked up to us and joined the conversation. Sarah, intuiting something was wrong, asked Theresa what the problem was. Theresa explained her fear of Katrina making a scene if she found her speaking to David. Sarah urged Theresa to go into the chapel and not to worry. So Theresa, emboldened by the two of us, walked in and began speaking in hushed words to her deceased former husband and lifelong friend. We left her to have her moment, the sound of her tearful farewell bubbling behind us.

Of course, Katrina instantly materialized, as if she had sniffed out a chance to make a scene. Seeing David's ex-wife alone with him, Katrina charged, arms swinging, in a rage toward Sarah.

"Who told her she could go in there?" Katrina asked, accusingly.

Sarah said, "hmm I'm not sure" and seeing in Katrina's glare that she wasn't satisfied with this answer, she added that maybe I had told Theresa she could. I didn't begrudge my sister for deflecting Katrina to me. We had a way of diffusing these confrontations. Katrina was too much blunt heat for either of us to impede alone. With a flap of her sails, Katrina changed direction and stormed toward me with added momentum. I looked away casually, intentionally aloof.

"Did you say Theresa could go in there?" she asked, less like a question, more like she had caught me.

In mock-ignorance, I shook my head, as if I had no clue what she was talking about.

"Maybe Sarah," I offered lackadaisically. She huffed and puffed and blew off, exasperated by this looping dead end to her investigation, by which point Theresa had had plenty of time to share her farewell in peace.

Katrina had her artful deception; we had our artful deflection. Any form of straightforward defense was futile against her aggression. Sarah and I exchanged winks across the room.

Later that evening, when most everyone was leaving or had already left, I took the opportunity to say some final words to David in the chapel where he laid. I tucked some pictures in with him: pictures of all of our siblings together, pictures of him with his kids.

I found a seat on one of the faded rose pews in the back of the chapel. Staring at the podium beside the casket, I wondered what tomorrow's funeral would be like, what the speakers might say, how many people might come. I needed to collect myself and let this new reality settle. The silence was piercing and fragile. I could have heard a strand of hair hit the carpet in that room. My ears rung with echoing silence, but they were soon relieved with soft footsteps.

From the back of the room, I watched as Sawyer walked into the chapel with a measured and leery gait, looking over his shoulder periodically as he approached. I knew him well enough to recognize this walk. He was not scared of the casket, as you might expect of such a young boy. No, what he feared threatened to come from behind him, hence his backward glances. He was scared of being caught by his mother.

I don't think he saw me, although it wasn't dark. The chapel was warmly lit with lamps and sconces. I felt that calling out to him would've been intrusive. He showed such courage walking in there alone. I considered how alone he must feel without his Daddy, the person in his life who had always been the peacemaker, the bridge-builder, the nurturer.

He walked up to the casket and stared into his Daddy's face. Then he bumped the casket with his elbow; it shook. He bumped it again, harder. It rocked on the stand. This was Sawyer's first confrontation with death. He was testing this strange reality, seeing if he could wake his Dad.

I remembered being that young—thinking everyone around you is how they always have been and that they will always be that way, forever. It's why pictures of a child's parents taken before they were born are so funny to them. With so few years of experience, time is more static, slower than it is for adults. To a child, it takes decades to get from this year's Christmas to next year's holiday. And to the adults: birthdays blur together, time accelerates without our approval, we forget our ages from time to time—unthinkable to a child whose every conquered year is a triumph of impossible patience.

Maybe I should keep him from rocking it. He could knock it over. But I couldn't justify such a trespass on Sawyer's moment with his Daddy.

The casket was bumped a few more times, not hard enough that it could fall but with enough force that I could see it moving, warbling under its own weight atop the stand as he tried to rouse David, testing what we had explained to him—that all of our bodies go to sleep forever one day, that David had gone to heaven. He was checking to see if this was true. His Daddy's body was here, but his Daddy was not. The paradox can be hard to accept, especially at six-years-old.

If Sawyer knocked it over, so be it. David wouldn't have minded, but Sawyer, now convinced by his test, walked away and out of the chapel as the casket wavered behind him.

The crowd at the funeral home the next day was too large to fit inside the building. Every pew was filled. All of the chairs in storage that Sawyer had hidden among were brought out, but there still weren't enough to accommodate everyone in attendance. People began standing against all the walls, in the aisles; soon there was no longer space to stand in the main room. Before long, the lobby was completely full as well. Two additional crowds gathered outside the entryways waiting to get in. So many flower arrangements were sent that the funeral home had to send trucks of them early to the gravesite to allow room for the flowers that continued piling in.

A wake of whispers followed Katrina as she made rounds of the crowd, as if socializing at a party that she was the life of, even in the midst of such an intimate death. This was her private masquerade. She wore the mask she always wore, and basked in this outpouring of undivided attention. With surgically painted makeup, never smudged by any mussing tears, she was the leading actress in this drama. As she drifted around in her shapeless black dress and espadrille shoes, a pairing she wore often, some were impressed by what they saw as enormous strength of spirit. A few pitying others thought she must be in a grave state of deep denial to feign such nonchalance, like she was postponing a suffering she hadn't yet confronted, but was inevitable, rising up like water behind a flimsy dam. They felt that she was icily unbothered because of the impending hell inside her, temporarily frozen over by aberrant tragedy. But the great majority of those whispers were from those discomforted by her chilly charm, those who were leery of this funerary extravert, acting so abnormally normal for a wife at her husband's funeral.

As the music began, I was shocked to hear that the first selection was a country song. David hated country music. This was no secret. But Katrina, who knew best that David hated country music, loved it. I tried not to dwell on this obvious jeer. I focused on other things, but then the next song was country, and the next—two Vince Gill songs and one by Lori Morgan.

These songs weren't appropriate for a funeral even if David had enjoyed country music. Katrina was doing everything she could to make this her movie, even supplying her own soundtrack, her score. Cheap melodrama had been crudely substituted for sanctity and respect for the wishes of the deceased.

David's best friends were seated behind me. Over my shoulder, I saw one of them shake his head repeatedly in disgust, another knuckled down on the edge of his chair in suppressed outrage. I could feel the heat of their rising anger on the back of my neck. This insult was intentional. She couldn't hurt David anymore, but she could hurt the ones who loved him.

After hearing these three unorthodox music selections, the funeral director asked my mother to choose a song. She chose "Amazing Grace", the only appropriate song of the service.

The funeral home offered limo service to my mother for the procession to the gravesite. Mom turned it down. But Katrina overheard one of my sisters telling another sister that Mom had refused the limo—it was typical of Mom. She wasn't showy. Like David, she felt gaudiness was cheap. Besides, a limo seemed too celebratory. Mom wasn't celebrating anything.

Katrina judged differently, she was jealous they hadn't offered the limo to her. She was the widow now, she was the one to be pitied, and this was her show. She went to the funeral director and demanded that she have the limo because she was the wife of the deceased.

The funeral director was already skeptical of her after having seen the scene she made at the hospital, denying an autopsy that the rest of the family wanted. And by now, he had new reasons to be skeptical of her. The preparation of David's body had been surprisingly difficult. It had required a triple-point injection of embalming fluid because of blocked circulatory passages. Men of his age, even victims of heart attacks, don't typically require a triple-point injection. In addition to this, David's hands were in a curious shape. They were cupped, as if frozen while clasping a cup or a pole. The funeral director was looking for the right time to explain this to our family.

Katrina's Mom, step-Dad, sisters, Lindsey and Sawyer, all rode in the limo. David and Theresa's daughter Madeline was excluded as usual.

Vehicles stopped as a sign of respect to allow our procession to pass by unimpeded on its way to the gravesite. I was moved by this as we drove. At one point, I saw we were approaching a convoy of military Humvees, all of them pulled over, and then they proceeded to get out of their vehicles, take off their hats and place them over their hearts as we passed. My eyes misted as we rolled slowly by the line of these service men and women.

When we arrived at the cemetery, Katrina stepped out of the limo and panned back and forth, sweeping the crowd, waiting for her arrival to be acknowledged like a celebrity arriving at a red carpet.

It was windy and sunny and those attending the graveside service hid behind reflective sunglasses. Leaves crunched underfoot. The breeze teased up the pungent perfume of damp soil and fermenting fallen foliage. Magnolia petals littered the cemetery grounds, some white and glinting in the sun while others browned like bites out of discarded apples. The air was as crisp as the leaves that chattered in the debris of autumn. Loose leaves were combed from the cemetery boughs with each fine-tooth gust and they piled up downwind, caught against a fence, creating a solid brown wall that trapped more leaves until the gust dropped them with held breath.

Sometimes the weather can be too nice.

This great loss was a mystery, a gaping enigma for all except Katrina who seemed fully recovered. The rest of the world hurdled on. We tried to move on with it.

A cold front rolled in the next day, chilly dry air filtered the yellow warmth out of the sunlight. For lack of any other thought of what to do with myself, I went to see Katrina. I wanted to see how she was doing. I needed to see her in distress, without an audience.

As I walked up to the house from the street in the blue light of dusk, I noticed a stray barn cat, dead at the corner of the property. I imagined some remorseful driver quietly pulling the animal out of the road and into the yard, thinking they had run over a family pet. *At least it was quick and clean*, I thought. I walked up the steps and noticed a balding brown patch in the grass just off from the porch. I imagined my brother furrowing the ground with a rake, sprinkling seed, saturating the soil with the hose to repair the patch to its rightful green.

Katrina, having heard my approach up the porch stairs, opened the door and let me in without my knocking. She didn't say anything, but that seemed appropriate. Her husband had been buried the day before. We stood in the kitchen a moment, then Katrina broke the silence, telling me how she was relieved there wasn't going to be an autopsy because she didn't want David's body to go through that kind of trauma. I said nothing. I had seen the argument play out in the hospital. I had heard of her sneaky sabotage of that resolution. I wanted no part in this rekindling of conflict. That's not what I had come for. In retrospect, I realize that my reticence made her nervous because she raised both of her hands in mock-surrender and said in a shaky cracked voice, uncharacteristic of her usual assertive, confrontational nature, "And there's no reason anyone would suspect me".

I assumed this type of practiced melodrama was another attempt to bait me into that argument over the cancelled autopsy. But I realized that she was fishing for my approval. In my silence I refused. She had usurped the wishes of family and friends for her own selfish preference. I still didn't understand why she preferred not knowing what happened to David.

Katrina walked out to the porch. I followed her. She began telling me that she had spoken with one of her friends. Her friend had told her that David was "just sleeping." Katrina said this made her feel good.

The idea that my brother was trapped in a permanent sleep was not comforting to me, although I didn't feel inclined to share that opinion with her. I generally avoided conflict with Katrina. I didn't understand how she found such an inconclusive ending to be comforting.

After the painful sight of my brother sealed, breathless in a bag, I had found a verse in Second Corinthians that I found comforting. 2 Corinthians 5:8 explains how being absent from the body is to be present with the Lord. I shared this with her. This verse expressed more eloquently what her friend's advice had tried, but failed in my mind, to provide. I did not share this in a hostile or argumentative way. I was far too emotionally exhausted to harbor any ulterior motive or embark on any holier-than-thou evangelizing. I merely shared what I found comforting, after she had shared what she found comforting. It was the natural course of the conversation. But my comment infuriated her. She didn't attempt to conceal or curb her irritation with me.

"Well, I don't believe half of what the Bible says," she said, incensed. I hadn't expected such anger, and I jumped. I was foolish enough to assume we were both suffering and sharing our struggle. Her supposed misery didn't allow fellowship, but required an audience of commiserates. I turned to look at her, to see the face that matched this outrage, but she looked away. When she did raise her face toward me it was like she was another person. She started laughing...

I left in a "nice hurry," perplexed as to why my benign comment had made her so giggling mad.

Days later my mother ran into the funeral director. He explained to Mom that they usually embalm with a single-point injection, but they had had to do a three-point injection due to heavy circulatory clotting. This man had been doing this work for decades and felt something was not right. Also, David's hands had been in rigid "C" shapes, like he had been gripping something cylindrical. The funeral director didn't know what had caused David's hands to get stuck in that peculiar grip.

They couldn't make his hands flatten without breaking the bones, so they left them curled that way and covered them for presentation in the casket. These oddities, along with Katrina's strange resistance to an autopsy, which he had seen first-hand at the hospital, all had the funeral director concerned. He had been mulling over these suspect quirks and had finally decided he had to tell our family. He encouraged my mother to look further into David's death.

Months went by and my parents grew increasingly irritated that the headstone had yet to be placed at David's resting place. Soon they discovered why. Katrina had refused to pay for any of the funeral expenses—not for the expensive triple-point embalming, nor a headstone, nor the limo service she had demanded. She refused to acknowledge any of the bills the funeral home sent her. She would not pay for any of the services even as she went ahead spending the insurance money that had been specifically set aside for such expenses.

She did not have the courtesy to inform my parents of her refusal. They were embarrassed when the funeral home called them about non-payment. Being honorable people, they felt this reflected poorly on them, but the funeral director assured them it was not their fault.

Unsure of the future, I looked back into memory in search of the missing pieces, to piece together a view of the big picture. My life was now irrevocably altered. Everyone was asking questions but there were no answers.

Chapter 3

Perryville is county seat and respective metropolis of Perry County—home to about 1500 people as of 2000. This landlocked community in this landlocked state is named after a naval hero who fought in the War of 1812, Commodore Oliver Hazard Perry.

The city website claims, "We are a Second Class City,"—their words, not mine.

We moved here from Chickasha, Oklahoma to be closer to my grandmother whose health was deteriorating. We have a lot of family here in Arkansas.

I was fifteen when we moved and as I took stock of my new surroundings I began to wonder why the leaders of Perryville named all these streets after letters and numbers. Sure, it was convenient, but why couldn't they have mixed in some more colorful names? Why not name the streets after local people or landmarks or choose themes like flowers or trees like I had seen in so many other neighborhoods?

Someone gave me an explanation. I am not sure it is entirely accurate, but I am positive it is true in a figurative way, at least.

I was told that originally all of the streets were named after the families that had lived here for generations. Their familiar names were scattered across the imperfect grid plan. These signs replaced the ancient white markers on street corners that were easily obscured by ditch grass.

Travelers were always getting lost. The city officials felt this gave visitors a bad impression. Hence, the motivation to modernize Perryville with new street signs.

The problem, the story goes, was that all of these signs were stolen within a few weeks. The running theory is that the Perryvillains stole them. Seeing one's surname on city property proved too great a temptation. It was something to hang on the wall; anybody who was anybody had one of their own. The community consensus was "why not?" Their tax dollars had paid for the signs; their names were stamped on them in bright refractive font.

Not all the thefts were for gloating or display, though. Some were for target practice—the name of some nuisance or rival nailed to a tree, hailed with rounds like a rural American voodoo doll.

For a time, Perryville had no street signage, all the stumpy white markers having been knocked down and grown over, or hauled away. These markers were speed bumps on the road to modernity. Although they had been labeled with the same names as the new signs, stealing them was never popular; maybe because they were so heavy, maybe because they didn't hang well on walls, or maybe Perryvillains hadn't noticed their names had been on them all along.

Locals tended to describe routes in the language of landmarks, anyway: Second left after Jones Family Restaurant, next right after Big Star Food and Drug.

In this absence of signage, anyone passing through was sure to get lost if they strayed far from the highway. Plenty of letters died in the mail, flying blind whenever piloted by the less experienced postal workers.

Peering from porches and convenience store windows, locals enjoyed a near-endless supply of disoriented cars circling block after block. It became a local pastime—how many times one could count the same vehicle lapping the cloistered city center. Perryvillains grinned, knowing that their community was not too small to get lost within.

This was the reputation that city officials had hoped to avoid. Their town was a "turn-around-place". They bought more new signs, shooting a second arrow to find the first, and they were confident this new plan would provide direction.

The streets were labeled with numbers and letters. No one loved or hated the signs. No one had any interest in them.

There were fewer cars to count circling the courthouse square, but drivers still confused Perryville with the neighboring town of Perry sometimes. As a child, I imagined some fraternal feud in the earliest days of Perry County, some bitter dispute mobilizing rival siblings to establish their own separate settlements abutting each other, divided by bad blood and a line drawn in the red dirt.

Perry County is no stranger to feuds and rival factions. As County Seat, Perryville has endured much of the collateral damage from these fallouts. The courthouse has been burned to the ground three times. The first fell to the Lively and McCool feud. The materials to build the second courthouse, already bought and paid for, rotted in the rain of the Civil War. All the men had left to fight; some blue, some gray. This tiny town was divided even in that national conflict, torn between the commercial interests of an upland timber economy and the dominance of cotton. The third courthouse burned when people became outraged over alleged election fraud. Any evidence of fraud was probably burned along with it. The fourth courthouse burned during a conflict that has come to be called "The Perry County War" in 1881. The fifth courthouse was built of brick and still stands in the square.

This area was once covered with virgin hardwood forest. Arcades of huge trees, like columns, instilled the sensation of being in a very old place. The quiet was punctuated by the creak and crack of shifting branches, or the applause of leaves. Intermittent sounds only sharpened the silences between them. You can feel a residual busyness in places like this—the stage traffic of human dramas that have come and gone, large and small, scenes and acts. This was the "Wild West" at a point in our national history.

Early settlers found the shallows hospitable near the forks of the Fourche-LaFave River. Riverboat paddlewheels clapped and puffed here with hunters, trappers, timber harvesters and hardy settlers aboard. This was as far as these steamboats could travel, even with their modified hulls and buoyant pontoons and teams of men with ropes and pulleys and hooks to free the steamers from sandbars and strainers.

This was the last stop. The same shallows that attracted the first settlers, now forced the boats to turn around. They brought manufactured goods and left with timber, bear oil and furs. People came and went. Some decided to stay. This came to be known as the "turn-around-place".

In the fall, the hillsides looked like mounds of mums and marigolds. Winter exposed the gnarly limbs of old oaks. Each spring brought new compositions of daffodils as the season's rains shifted their bulbs through the soft soil into new arrangements. A patch of daffodils lifted from a ditch and planted proudly near the porch might spring up insolently in the middle of the yard. In summer, the longest season, collars wilted in the heavy valley heat by mid-morning. Dust hung suspended.

Regular steamboat service continued until the railroad tracks were laid to the north of Perryville, but the railroad failed to bring the growth and prosperity it had promised. A flicker of growth was ushered by the crackling asphalt of the highway laid to the east. But Perryville was eventually marginalized, once again, by the warp and woof of the new interstate's path which avoided the hills that rippled out of the Ouachitas.

Today, this small town is no less stratified for being miniscule; in fact, its social gradations are more intimate, and concentrated. Gossip is a performance art and social currency. Much has changed but more has remained the same. Sod and soybeans have replaced cotton fields in the river bottoms. The hillsides were shaved by early cut-and-run timber companies and remained bald until they were replanted with commercial pine divisions persist. Fourche River Days is still celebrated every spring. Perryville remains a "turn-around-place" but rather than the shallows, a less visible obstacle now impedes the outsider.

Here and there, a house fire raises a specific suspicion, not necessarily a gas leak, or bad wiring, or a cigarette fallen from a chapped lip, but possibly the explosion of some hill-chemist's lab after a flawed measurement or sloppy execution. These concoctors and their fires are some derivative of another era's bootleggers—building volatile stills, and tasting batches that could blind them.

Driving into and out of town, both of which can be done in only a matter of minutes, the highways meander between hairpin turns along the stitches of ridges between the quilted croplands, past yards strewn with truck and tractor parts, retired machines and sinking appliances. They are clutter to the passerby, but the gaps left where parts have been removed show that they have proved useful. These are the telltale signs of that uniquely rural resourcefulness.

At the same time, scattered more sparsely, a few large houses stand, the centerpieces of auspiciously manicured lawns with their stripes of carefully mowed alternating greens in defiance of the rough pasture or furrowed farmland or tangled forest surrounding them. There is something modestly poetic and quietly heroic in this spectrum of hardworking people, in their earnestness, and grit.

This is the same small southern show that Hollywood embraces with cliché. The locals perform their assigned roles so perfectly, so genuinely, that they parody themselves. This is a place where people you've just met tell you to "come on by sometime" but don't actually intend to find you on their porch; it's just what people say. The local flavor of conversation is friendly to figurative language, full of elaborate fibs and short simple truths. It's recreation to share a re-creation.

Like people everywhere, Perryvillains enjoy distinguishing themselves from communities around them, whether through local sports or county beautification projects. Rivalries can get bitter for their proximity. Towns quarrel like siblings that have forgotten how much they have in common. In reality people live similar lives. They work and struggle. They hope and doubt. They love and lose and repair. For all of Perryville's difference and indifference to the world outside it, it is a microcosm of everywhere.

I do not believe that small towns suffocate aspirations or squelch spirits or stunt imaginations. On the contrary, I am convinced that such places can be ideal for incubating greatness in some. Some bloom where they are planted and some shift to soil more appropriate for their growth, like daffodils swimming through the soil from season to season.

But small towns can also insulate and concentrate social ailments in a unique way. Small towns can give small-minded people the inflated illusion that they are big fish as they swim tight recursive circles in a small pond.

Perhaps Katrina thought herself a big fish. She may consider herself "the one that got away," but such notoriety is double-edged. Everyone wants to catch the big fish, although she may look smaller out of water.

Chapter 4

I have heard several accounts of how Katrina and David met, and like a shoebox of snapshots they cobble together a collage of that night. Our family was just about to move from Chickasha, Oklahoma to Perryville, Arkansas.

David was newly divorced from his first wife, Theresa. They had had a daughter together, Madeline. David and Theresa still got along and remained genuine friends, but they realized they had made a mistake. The separation was still difficult, despite their mutual respect. They had just been too young, David guessed.

David's friends had succeeded in getting him out of his house that night. He was a workaholic in the oil fields of Oklahoma at the time. He was always taking on extra hours and volunteering to fill in for others' absences. When he did get off work he was a homebody, always staying in and working on carpentry projects or miscellaneous repairs. That was how David dealt with things; he just worked harder. His friends tried to get him to relax and realize he had more life ahead of him than behind him. He was young, only twenty-one. They went out to play pool and have drinks at a sports bar in Chickasha that night.

A woman walked in and stopped by the pool table. She stared at my brother, waiting for his attention. The other guys noticed this, but David was too invested in the shot he was lining up to notice until one of his friends ribbed him. It was obvious to all of them who this woman had her eyes on; lust at first sight.

David looked up and their eyes met. He smiled politely and went back to his shot, not thinking much of it. He was glad to be out with friends again. He was not looking for anything more complicated than a few games of pool.

After a long stare, Katrina walked out of the room to the patio dining area of the restaurant.

The guys erupted after she had left. "Whoa, man, what was that? I think you've got an admirer!" they jeered. David laughed it off, flattered but disinterested.

A few minutes later, David received a drink with a note on the napkin. The guys broke into laughs and claps and knee slaps.

The note read, "Come outside to the dining area to meet the woman you're going to spend the rest of your life with. I'm going to make all your fantasies come true starting tonight, Katrina, XOXO"

The inky letters bled into the napkin as it dampened with condensation.

David was a little wary of this advance. He wondered if she felt the need to write that grandiose note because he had ignored her. She must have felt snubbed, he thought.

David's friends assured him this was just a lucky break; he should learn to accept good things. They suggested that he at least join her for that drink, no harm in that.

"It's only polite," David acquiesced.

He had a few drinks with her. It was a welcome diversion. He was refreshed by the freedom of a first conversation, the liberating lack of history between them, no baggage. But there was no chase in this chance romance, only easy acceptance and the warmth of a few empty glasses.

Katrina wound up at David's house in Chickasha that night. Afterward, he realized almost immediately that this sudden arrangement was not sustainable. Freshly divorced, he had been caught on the rebound. He didn't really know this woman. At first, this mystery had been pleasantly new, but now it was full of variables.

He had a daughter to think of; Madeline needed stability. He needed to focus on being a Dad for a while. This was not the time to jump into a long-term relationship which Katrina had already proclaimed was her goal.

Katrina was persistent, aggressive even, while her communication, beginning with that napkin note, was almost child-like in its playground tone of fantasy. It reminded him of grade school love notes with a YES or NO to circle.

She said "I love you" when they had just met, meaning she either didn't fully understand what those words mean or she didn't mean what she was saying. She was either too naïve or too vapid to feel the weight of those words.

All of us except for David had just left Oklahoma for Arkansas. With some hard-won earnings saved up and his divorce finalized, David was preparing to follow us. It was important to him to be close to family. He anticipated a career change and a fresh start.

At this juncture he had no intention to fray new loose-ends in Chickasha. He already regretted wandering into this entanglement. There was no sense in prolonging this short-fuse fling any longer.

Despite his apologetic and honest explanation that he was in a transitional chapter of his life, that he could not begin a new relationship in good faith, that he had a daughter to think of, that his family had moved away and he was joining them in Arkansas, Katrina was not predictably sad or disappointed, she was infuriated.

She argued vehemently that she had a daughter too, as if this negated his reasons for leaving, like she could debate him into staying. She became even clingier, more smothering. She was four years older than David.

Katrina couldn't believe it when David began making moving arrangements a few days later. She was inflamed by the prospect of David being "the one that got away." David was a good catch: young, handsome, healthy, and financially independent. Katrina left his house in a storm. The sight of David packing was the only thing that had succeeded in getting her out of the house. It was over as quickly as it had begun.

David hated that it had to end this way. Why couldn't she understand? He had sincerely explained everything considerately to Katrina. He expected more maturity. It wasn't as if he had plotted to pick her up then coldly dropped her. She had approached him.

This instant baggage assured him that he was doing the right thing by moving on. The need to preserve new possibilities for his life was reaffirmed by this short and disproportionately complicated relationship.

A month or so later, just days before David moved away from Chickasha, he got an unexpected call from Katrina. She was pregnant. She insisted that she should move with him to Arkansas.

David was steeped in stress. His conscience was torn with guilt. What had he gotten himself into? Always responsible, David figured this served him right for his lapse in judgment. The most logical way to accept this turbulence in his life was in the form of penance, like a monkish vow. He decided to accept this boldly and honorably, to sail with this wind of change in the direction it provided. David's relationship with Katrina wasn't over after all.

A shotgun wedding loaded with happenstance was hastily planned between them. It didn't require a shotgun in David's back to coerce him to walk down that aisle. His own conscience was a sharp prod.

They hurried through the hushed ceremony. It was a private affair, at the pastor's house. None of their family or friends were invited.

David was unsure of this new course his life was taking. He regretted that foggy night and the new complications it brought, but he could only regret for so long; he had to move forward. In order for life not to be something that just happens *to* you, one has to make decisions and claim some piloting agency, without that steering Will we are all leaves clinging against the wind, waiting for something to happen, aimless when it does.

This wasn't what he expected to be doing so soon after his recent divorce. He was trying to do the right thing—for this unborn child and for the reputation of this woman that walked into his life. He had to believe this was happening for a reason. He had to believe this was part of some greater plan.

David brought Katrina from Chickasha to my parent's house in Perryville, along with his two-year-old daughter. He introduced Katrina as his new bride.

We were all surprised, but tried not to look surprised so they wouldn't feel uncomfortable. I could tell that Mom felt his resolve to "do this right" was redeeming, chivalrous. She was proud of him, yet she was worried that his good-nature might be exploited by this mysterious woman.

The seed of guilt that Katrina had planted in him when he had tried to leave was developing into a self-deprecating sense of duty. He had been drafted for this mission by his own conscience.

After everyone seemed properly acquainted, David left the room for a moment. In his absence, I watched as Katrina did something strange, something so absurd that it caused me to doubt my eyes at first, because what I saw so vastly deviated from my expectation. Katrina turned toward young Madeline and scrunched her face into a teeth-bearing snarl. It was not an expression of play or pain but a face intended to intimidate or unsettle. The twinkle momentarily left Madeline's blue eyes, her constant giggle paused, her cheeks, always lifted high by the corners of her smile, fell slack. Her bright blonde hair fell from a toddler's happy bounce to stillness; but Madeline did not cry.

Katrina had made the face a child gives another when the teacher isn't looking; in this case, between an adult and a two-year-old. It was the nonverbal language that signals a persisting grudge, unfinished business to be settled on some playground later. I don't think she realized I saw her.

But then I wondered if she *had* seen my reaction to her, because when David returned to the living room she immediately hopped onto the floor and began baby-talking to Madeline so loudly that soon all the clusters of conversations lulled as our family was drawn as an audience to this performance of cloying kindness. This change in her was so abrupt that I wondered if she realized I had seen her sour snarl and if this scripted scene was the cover-up to discredit anything I might tell our family, which she was now strangely a part of.

Katrina teased at her own bangs in the stage light of our family's attention, exposing the dark roots of her false blonde. Madeline went along amiably with the show, a hint of caution apparent in the curbed enthusiasm of this typically smiley little girl.

I am the youngest of seven. Youngest siblings see more than they are given credit for, more than their elders realize. If you are quiet long enough, people forget you are there. Our youth puts doubt in our accounts, but because people believe we are unlikely to be heard, they fail to keep their masks on in our presence. Youth matures, and holds on to those puzzle pieces to assemble later.

David smiled at Katrina and his daughter and walked back to the kitchen. I followed him out with some vague idea that I had to tell him what I had seen. But I thought better of it. I realized my well-meant disclosure would not be happily received after the show everyone had just seen in the living room. It could be dangerous to be the messenger of such uncomfortable news. To share my suspicion I needed more evidence, more purpose for what this disclosure would accomplish. And what would it accomplish? Even if everyone believed me and felt something should be done, what could be done? That tantrum wasn't enough to make this entrapping pregnancy or hasty marriage disappear. The certain cost outweighed the ambiguous benefit, so I kept what I saw to myself.

My brother turned to me as I joined him in the kitchen. I could tell he had missed Mom's cooking as he browsed among what Mom had prepared, "grazing" we joked. Out of earshot from everyone else he asked me, in a hushed tone, "Do you like her?"

I decided then that I did not want to create a divide between us. That tiny shred of self-doubt was too large for me to risk my relationship with him.

Settling for lukewarm propriety, I kept my true reservations to myself. But I would have to condense this half-hearted concession into just one word or my real opinion might escape and offend him.

"Yes," I answered plainly. I knew he was doing his best.

After Katrina became her daughter-in-law my mother looked for opportunities to spend time with Katrina, trying to get to know her in an accelerated fashion. Mom also helped Katrina find a job at the company where she was the quality control supervisor.

One Saturday evening, Mom invited everyone over for dinner and conversation. We talked while dinner was cooking.

The short sleeves of Katrina's shirt revealed a large scar striped across her shoulder. Mom noticed and asked about it. Mom was curious and happy for a conversation piece. Mom had discovered that Katrina liked to tell stories.

Katrina said she had been an officer on the Chickasha Police force and had been shot in the shoulder. Hearing that she had been an officer was a relief to my mother, something solid about this stranger's past. Personally, I was impressed, possibly even impressed enough to wash my memory of that face she had stabbed at Madeline; it was easier to believe I hadn't seen it. She had been shot! Wow! I was fifteen and this tale was an inspiring ode to girl power in my young opinion. I felt associated with a courageous celebrity. We were all impressed, and somewhat reassured.

A few weeks later, I returned to Chickasha for a weekend to visit a friend at her parent's house. It had been hard to leave friends behind. Of course, that wild story I had just been told was on the tip of my tongue. I had to tell my friend about my new sister-in-law getting shot in the line of duty. I delivered the tale with as much cinematic narration as I could. My friend was impressed. I knew she would be. It can be exhilarating to share a story you're privy to. It was such an incredible story; I had to do it justice in my retelling.

My awestruck friend asked if the shooting happened in Perryville. I explained that Katrina was shot in Chickasha while serving on their police force. After I said this my friend's father stepped out from the kitchen.

"I used to be an officer here. What's her name? Maybe I know her."

"Katrina" I told him proudly.

His eyebrows raised; he started laughing. I thought maybe he didn't think girls should be officers, that they weren't tough enough, that they would get shot. I was growing righteously annoyed with him. I expected a former officer to show more respect for an injured colleague.

He caught his breath. "That lady was a dispatcher. She never patrolled. No way she ever got shot."

He hiccupped a few more laughs. "You better tell your brother to stay away from that one."

My friend was awkwardly silent. I didn't know what to say. Her father didn't either. He walked back into the kitchen as if he felt he had said too much. It was clear he knew more about her than he was willing to tell me. I wanted to ask, but I doubted if he would divulge anymore. I was a curious teenager, unsure what to think and embarrassed by this unraveled story

Once again, I found myself torn between action and inaction. What, if anything, could I do with this latest revelation about Katrina? I wanted to take this man's advice and tell David to stay away from her but I was certain David would hear it as gutter gossip if I didn't disclose the credible source who had revealed Katrina's deception. Otherwise, David might assume I was just trying to discredit her story. Even if I told David who told me, a grudge between my brother and my friend's Dad wouldn't make anyone's life easier, least of all mine. What would I gain by attempting to expose Katrina's lie about a pretend battle wound? She was no longer impressive. I felt duped and silly after having just proudly told what I thought was a truly heroic story.

It was senseless of her to breed such a blockbuster lie. I found it pathetic more than anything, pitiful, like a child's expansive bragging but lacking a child's redeeming innocence. It wasn't necessarily a dangerous lie, but it was certainly suspicious.

Her lie was later exposed without me having to blow the whistle. Mom found out that the scar was from a surgery. Katrina's sister brought it up of her own volition in the course of a conversation. My mother hadn't even asked. Katrina's sister had no idea we had already been told an alternate version of the story.

Why fabricate such a dramatic lie? Did she have that story planned before Mom asked her about it or did she make it up on the spot, compulsively, tempted by every question to exploit people's trust toward some self-congratulation? Was it to impress us, was she that desperate? Or was it to intimidate us? Did she lie out of boredom to forge some fictitious excitement in her life? I couldn't rationalize any of these motives. I wondered if she was trying to hide something, but if that was the case why craft such sensational stories?

This enigmatic lie installed elephants in rooms whenever our extended family spent time together. But a few weeks passed and many of us lost interest as impending reality reminded us all that this woman was inexplicably a part of our family now and was soon to bring a new family member into the world.

Less than a month later, a much greater lie surfaced, not only pathetic but dangerous. The acid of this exposure dissolved the tenuous glue holding the whole fast and nasty arrangement together.

Chapter 5

Only a few weeks after she had moved to Perryville with David, Katrina announced that she had miscarried. She used this situation to milk maximum sympathy from everyone, but especially David. She rang her proverbial bell incessantly. He answered every beckoning call. He took off work to stay with her, always there to answer every need. All his attention was focused on her. He stopped answering the phone. She wouldn't allow company.

My sister Sarah had suffered the trauma of a miscarriage before. She ran into David at a local store. He was picking up things for Katrina. Sarah offered to go comfort Katrina. Sarah felt she could help because she knew what Katrina was experiencing. David said that he would ask Katrina if she would like that.

David called Sarah later that evening.

"No thanks, Katrina doesn't feel like talking. She's still just too upset."

This pity parade continued for weeks. David ran around trying to keep her appeased and fully comfortable. It was over the top. I don't intend to downplay the seriousness of a miscarriage whatsoever, but her actions became counterfeit feeling, so grossly melodramatic and transparently self-serving that her behavior cheapened the suffering of others like Sarah. She arrogantly put her suffering on a pedestal above others'.

Mom was exhausted with watching her son scramble around for Katrina who was increasingly excluding the rest of our family. Finally, Mom confronted David about it. It had become too painful to go on watching.

"This isn't healthy. It's time to move on. There's no need to ignore your family."

"She's just having a hard time, Mom. I don't want to hurt her after what she's been through."

Annoyed, my mother asked him, "Who is her doctor?"

David didn't recall hearing the doctor's name.

"Okay, what clinic then?"Mom asked.

He wasn't sure.

"When did she miscarry?"

He didn't know.

"Did she go to the doctor immediately? What did she do?"

He couldn't say.

He didn't have an answer to any of these basic questions about the miscarriage.

When David got home he asked Katrina for some details. He called Mom the next day. Katrina had told him that her doctor was Dr. May in Morrilton but she also said she didn't go to the doctor when she miscarried because there was nothing the doctor could have done.

This did not make sense to Mom. She had a bad feeling about all this; some alarm of motherly instinct was going off, alerting her that something was not right.

Mom finally decided to tell David that she didn't believe Katrina. She begged him, "Please get away from her NOW while you have nothing holding you to her."

Calm came over Mom's face when David told her that he was getting away, but this just wasn't the right time. I believe they were mutually relieved; David, that Mom wouldn't be disappointed in him if he got a divorce, and Mom, that this woman had fallen from her son's favor, and had been revealed to him as something other than what she appeared.

"I'll be okay, Mom," he said.

The next day, Mom and I spent hours exhaustively calling all hospitals and clinics in the area. There were no doctors with the surname "May." That confirmed everyone's suspicion about the ghost pregnancy. Katrina had never been pregnant. She had succeeded in pressuring David into a hurried marriage. This deception was far more destructive than an exaggerated scar story.

Mom was relieved in a roundabout way, because her son was no longer bound to this woman by his own exploited empathy. Still, Mom hated to see him suffer. David was crushed, conned. It was psychologically and emotionally devastating. David felt like a fiddle, his strings plucked, and played. The tumbling tailspin continued.

It was over. They separated. He filed for divorce.

We all breathed easier, feeling a strange and rushed chapter had finally come to its fiery fallout.

Katrina had so ingratiated herself to David that I feared it required something of this magnitude to brush the scales from his eyes.

Although I hated to see David hurt, it was a necessary evil. I cringed, imagining what else might have happened if he had been stuck with her, never realizing he was being manipulated. It was better this happened now rather than later in some absurdly compounded state. The longer it went on the more he would have believed her, like an attachment to a depreciating investment because he had already invested so much.

When Katrina came out of her hiding after this gross charade I was surprised to see that the belly I had assumed was the first sign of pregnancy still remained—a convenient prop I supposed.

After the separation, David began acting like himself again. He kept company with friends and family. He fished and played basketball at the gym. Eventually, he even began casually seeing a new girl. Mom was happy to see him happy and moving on. She felt this was a good sign. He was coming out of Katrina's corrosive anesthesia. It felt like normalcy was returning. I was going to take David up on his next fishing invitation.

But Katrina didn't leave quietly. She needed to reclaim the stage. She had the nerve, after this disgusting life-altering pregnancy lie, to vocally accuse David of cheating on her with this new girl he was seeing well after their separation.

Katrina assumed the role of an embattled damsel in distress. She twisted facts like soft dough, put them in her charismatic furnace and half-baked them into a performance.

Katrina confused people as a social berserker. She reacted to people who were offended by her by making a show of being more offended by them for being offended. Anyone absently polite enough to ask how she was doing would get the whole sensational diatribe.

This accusation of adultery made no sense to anyone because they were no longer together. Don't you have to be in a relationship in order to cheat? We were coming to find that this rancid reasoning was typical of her. Most of us expected that Katrina was on her way out of town. She had no ties in Perryville other than David and that connection was severed.

She had exploited David's noblest qualities, his selflessness and empathy, to trick him into a marriage he didn't want. As her theatrics continued to pollinate rumors, we put her out of mind, knowing, at least, that David was free of her and she would soon be gone. Soon they would be legally divorced and she could no longer haunt David.

But with a sour twist of fate, Katrina came back into David's life a few months later, and as a result, into my life as well. Just before the divorce papers were finalized, she claimed to be pregnant once again. The absurdity continued with this surreal déjà vu. David demanded proof, a pregnancy test. Strangely enough, she was pregnant. Katrina was going to bring another human being into the world, into our family. This festering rash on our family life couldn't be alleviated. David was stuck on her emotional rollercoaster. And we too were tethered along to this nauseating ride by our heartstrings.

Katrina told David that if he left her, he would never see the child. David couldn't stand to have a child out in the world with no knowledge of him. He couldn't allow that to burden his conscience for the rest of his life, as he knew it surely would. He knew this threat was not empty. She would make sure he never saw this child. He was positive of this because he knew she had already succeeded in shutting out a father of one of her children once before. Katrina's daughter Lindsey had no idea who her father was. None of us did. Katrina had begun telling Lindsey that David was her father. He was the only father she would come to know.

They negotiated as if still in the middle of a divorce, except that it was full of conditions contingent on David staying rather than leaving. Their relationship had never been what I would call "normal," but after this string of deceptions and threats, they shared a marriage in name only, a sterile legal bond.

David forgave her for shattering his trust; he just wanted it to be over. He did his best to move forward with a marriage that was exclusively contractual. He didn't know what else there was to do. As was his habit, he took the high road and let it go, hoping to diffuse the conflict. He was averse to conflicts. They drained him. He simply didn't want to continue investing his energy maintaining grudges, keeping score, stoking flames, yet Katrina seemed to thrive off conflict. She craved it like a drug. She needed one as often as she needed a cigarette. Conflict stimulated her. After an awkward confrontation she appeared refreshed while others, weary and wary, tiptoed around her. David's sweet southern chivalry and his warmth made him malleable to her surgical manipulation. He was her favorite game piece.

David was well aware that judges often rule in favor of the mother regarding custody, especially in cases involving newborns. Divorcing a pregnant woman would ensure that all sympathy fell in her corner. He knew it would be quite a performance. She would love the chance at an audience on a courtroom set. She was toxic, but David couldn't allow himself to be a man who had fathered a child unknown to him. His conscience wouldn't allow it.

It began to seem as though Katrina didn't have any such conscience to constrain her impulses or motivate any compassion. She carried herself guiltlessly, even proudly, as if she had won some sick contest. David was her indentured prize. She wasn't even embarrassed after having two huge lies exposed. She loved the attention.

In her coldly controlling negotiations with David, she was swollen with pride as she laid out uncompromising conditions like a power-broker making an asymmetric deal. Like a slimy politician she conceded scandal as a sign of her strength. She possessed far more cunning than virtue.

This was not the life David had planned, but by now he was keenly aware how vulnerable even the best laid plans are. This thin-lipped, hyphen-eyed woman was making him feel like a mouse. He set his mind to making lemonade with this bitter lemon that life had handed him, a lemon that required constant maintenance yet could never be depended on. He anticipated the arrival of a little bundle of sugar to temper this lemon's sour—thus, lemonade would be made. He even hoped this little person might weld their relationship back together and repair what had always been broken.

Although David forgave her, as hard as that must have been, Katrina refused to forgive him for "cheating" when they had been separated. At first, I was angry that David had forgiven her, but I came to realize this clear-headedness was one of the reasons I respected him so much. I couldn't fault him for thinking of his family's future. He was wise beyond his years; his slightly receding hairline and distinguished deep brown eyes gave credence to this wisdom despite his youthful face. He was thinking of the kids, after all, and I admired him for staying above the fray for them. They lived in an unpredictable atmosphere; they were always on edge. This stress took a toll on them and I understood David's refusal to add volatility to their lives. But to hear after all of David's reasonableness—that she refused to forgive *him*, made me nauseous. Katrina insisted on calling it "cheating," although I doubt most people would consider his mild socializing as adultery, given the absurd context. He had already filed for divorce after being conned into marriage under false pretenses.

Katrina never stopped accusing David of cheating. When she ought to have been the one feeling guilty, she bullied him into a guilt trip. She cheated his good nature. How could she be so shamelessly hypocritical? It was as if she had no self-awareness, no clue or care for how people perceived her.

Shortly before baby Sawyer was born, my aunts and I were sitting with Katrina and talking. My aunts had been carefully organizing small get-togethers hoping to subtly mend the ties that had been broken with Katrina. It was clear she wasn't leaving anytime soon. My aunts didn't want to forfeit their relationship with this nephew they were anticipating. And after the way Katrina had monopolized David during the entire miscarriage stunt, we didn't want to give her any reason to exclude us. It was strange, I thought, for everyone to tolerate this deceiver in hopes that she wouldn't exclude them. Even after she was known to be a liar, she was still exerting influence.

The conversation wasn't exactly riveting, but my aunts were being sweet and polite as they always were and Katrina was adeptly playing along with her chatty style of shallow small talk, plastic smiles and self-congratulating anecdotes. Her sentiments always sounded as if she were reading them out of a phrase book. Emotion was a second language to her.

The forced conversation ebbed as it often does when people gather together for the sole purpose of getting along. In the space of that small silence, Katrina seemed to change characters before us, as if switching roles in a play. She broke the silence with a changed voice, and tore off on a tirade about wanting to "get David back for what he did." We were shell-shocked, unsure what had sparked this fury.

"Get him back for what?" one of my aunts asked, confused and concerned.

"He cheated on me and will pay for it one day," Katrina blustered.

Of course, we all knew David had not cheated on her. He had left her following her egregious life-altering lie. What sympathy did she expect to find in us? We were trying to forget what she had done; why wasn't she? Our cool reception wasn't enough to stop her from carrying on. She did not get the hint in our silence. She was woven into our lives by this irrefutable pregnancy. I expected her to be content by now. She now had my brother trying to do the right thing for this baby. Wasn't this what she had been finagling for all along? Hadn't she already won? Evidently, this was not enough.

One of my aunts asked Katrina to "please calm down. This is silly talk, honey" she said. "You two are starting a family together. You and David are together. It is time to move forward, Katrina. Put that behind you for your little ones."

Katrina's face reddened with heat rising from beneath. "I just want him to realize what he has done."

"What do you mean by that?" my aunt asked.

"You know what I mean!" Katrina hissed.

I didn't understand. Didn't she get what she wanted, what she had even lied for? She had David, and a baby to retain him, but now she was mad that she *was* pregnant. Her hot irrational temper was leading me to understand why people sometimes say "madness" in place of "crazy" or "insane."

Another aunt attempted to diffuse the tension in the room.

"Now Katrina, your body is undergoing a lot of changes right now, as you know. A child brings new stresses and worries, but I assure you everything is going to be fine."

Katrina just stared at her indignantly before carrying on.

"I don't really like kids. I didn't really want any," she barked.

In the back of everyone's mind was the fact that not long before this, Katrina had fabricated an entire false pregnancy. By this point, even my most docile aunt couldn't stand any more of this show.

"Well, what are you going to do?" she asked Katrina. "You're pregnant. You're married to David. Isn't this what you wanted? Why are you saying this?"

"Well, I'll deal with this one, but I don't *want* them," Katrina answered dismissively.

I was stunned by the wild things coming out of her mouth. It was all so manic and nonsensical. It was difficult to react to her with anything other than silence. There was no way to rationally respond to her belligerence.

My sweet aunt's description of how pregnancy alters hormones and emotions seemed like a huge understatement in my teenage mind. Evidently, pregnancy knocked you completely off your rocker. As her rant escalated, I watched as my aunts grew increasingly uncomfortable. Seeing these wise women, my mentors, grow visibly uneasy worried me.

If anyone attempted to interject and diffuse the tension Katrina trumpeted over them, continuing her filibuster. I wanted to change the subject, but I kept quiet through many awkward silences that day, surviving several eye-avoiding moments as Katrina made innumerable inflammatory statements that nobody in the room could believe or respond to. Everyone let their eyes wander around the floor or ceiling, glancing at anything besides Katrina, who scanned the room between examinations of her manicured nails, which despite her obsession, were still tinged nicotine-orange.

We didn't want to respond, or participate in the bullying charade, but we didn't want any of her fireworks either, so my aunts took shifts nodding and saying "uh huh" to avoid the ever-present conflict. This conversation was nourishing only to Katrina's ego.

Anytime her statements were questioned, when inconsistencies were exposed, or when she inadvertently contradicted herself, her eyes would go to the ceiling as she pretended to search her memory while she made up the rest of the story on the spot. Should anyone point out one of these episodes to be less than accurate, she might attack them about something entirely unrelated, or launch a charm-offensive, a flood of flattery and false benevolence to anesthetize. Her glib charm was entrapping.

If anyone got too close to the truth, or more often lack thereof, she would break down and make such a scene that no one in good conscience could continue trying to expose what lay beneath her fabric of both trivial and ruinous lies.

At first I had been awed by her cinematic claims, but by now I had noticed that these stories were often contradictory and the unrealistic variety and quantity of them made me doubt everything she said.

Anyone else would have left after this tirade but Katrina stayed. Here she had a captive audience. It was as if she sought out conflict for conflict's sake like some sadistic social game. She just wanted to watch us jump and tiptoe around her. Watching people scramble or mumble dejectedly validated her agency in the world.

It was remarkable to see such a cocktail of charisma and mania. That energy gave her a sort of animal magnetism. Katrina is interesting in the way a car wreck is interesting. She attracted rubberneckers.

She could be very funny—it was the only thing David could enjoy about her company—but her humor was typically self-congratulating. She gained laughs by making others feel small and simple and stupid. Her conversation was designed to exaggerate her supposed strengths and expose others' perceived weaknesses. It was a zero-sum game.

She could smell self-consciousness. She exploited insecurities with cheap stabs, then diffused the insulted person by saying something recalcitrant like "it's just a joke," or "don't take everything so seriously," or "we're friends, right?" Katrina retracted her claws with a voice of mock-meekness to make people feel as if they were over-reacting, as if the provoked were the provocateur. Katrina might then roll her eyes confidingly toward some other individual present, drawing her to smile in magnetic compliance. "What's her problem?" Katrina might ask in a loud stage whisper, forging another tiny alliance to draw upon later. She always wanted her hand on peoples' dials, turning them up, turning them down—attack, diffuse, ally, betray.

Katrina was good at this. She could get people to apologize for her having insulted them. She could cause warm genuine people to feel outrageous for being outraged by her playground tactics.

She was magnetic in the way many bad relationships are; people felt a need to be accepted by the person who made them feel weakest even if that search for acceptance meant staying in harm's way.

Only her acceptance held the illusion of repairing one's damaged esteem. She operated as a gatekeeper to the self-perceptions of others—an adult bully graduated to a professional playground.

Katrina's rant at my aunts passed at a glacial pace even as it heated to a boil. I wondered if this expected child was actually David's. Now she had this baby to bind David to her. She had my brother's obligation, what else did she want?

In hindsight, I realize that was the day her threats began.

Chapter 6

When baby Sawyer arrived I could no longer question whose son he was. Sawyer was David's spitting image. It was striking and gave me hope for some reason. Maybe things were coming together. Seeing David's resemblance in this brand new beautiful boy provided some comfort. It was a pattern in the midst of this chaos.

When Mom and I walked into the maternity ward to see Sawyer for the first time, David hugged us simultaneously around our necks, squeezing the three of us together. "I finally got my boy!" he said.

He told us it was one of the happiest days of his life. His face beamed with pure joy. His deep brown eyes were luminous. A wide smile stilted his cheeks.

For the next several years David and Katrina frequently asked me to babysit. I enjoyed spending time with the three kids—Madeline, Lindsey, and now Sawyer. It was a way to stay close to David and his kids.

When I was asked to watch them, my brother usually took his boat out to fish. "That's where I get my thinking done," he'd say. Or he would go to the gym to work out or play basketball with a group of his friends. He even began hunting, although he never had before. I joked with him that he might bring home more antlers if he spent his hunting weekends driving up and down the highways rather than sitting in a deer stand in the woods. All the strategy and stalking that went into fruitless hunts was funny to me since it was common to see a trophy rack punctured into the shaved-ice glitter of a shattered windshield. He joked along with me, calling me "punk" which was his particular endearment, but we both knew why he really went hunting. He didn't necessarily go fishing to catch fish, or hunting to harvest game. He needed to have places to go, to get away, and I understood that without him having to spell it out.

He couldn't spend a weekend at home without being on call for Katrina. Unless he made plans she would schedule his every hour. His honey-do lists were indentured work orders complete with deadlines and a supervisor wife to keep him on task. He did his best to avoid Katrina when possible but not at the expense of forfeiting time with his kids whom he took every opportunity to whisk away to visit family, ride bikes or join him on excursions to parks and lakes.

Periodically, he took Sawyer along on his fishing trips. To preclude the accusation of intentionally excluding her, David always invited Katrina as well. But she didn't have any interest in fishing and it wasn't because of the grossness of worms, or her empathy for minnows, as in the case of Lindsey and Madeline who weren't fond of fishing. Katrina teased the girls for not having the guts to put a hook through a minnow.

The only fishing Katrina did was for compliments. She fished her prey with careful phrases. She baited her self-flattering hooks with sycophant self-deprecations. "Oh please excuse me, I look just awful today." And she waited for a bite—to affirm whatever her vanity of the minute happened to be. She fished to feed her insatiable ego. She was needy but indifferent to the needs of others.

David found it easier to digest the indifference of honest sport, of fish that refused to bite, of a robbed jump shot. This variable was part of the game, an unknown that could make a game joyfully unpredictable. This variable allowed underdogs to upset experts, and kept the best players humble, fueling them to continue improving. These games, variables included, had structure, rules, and parameters to operate within. David could win and lose by the same variable and in that way the unknowns were fair—the same chance for everyone. For all the robbed shots, he had days of back to back three-pointers. He enjoyed the ball's peculiar way of getting caught for a particle of a second in the back of the net, mid-swoosh.

David found success in his work and play because he worked and played hard. His work ethic and sheer grit gave him a fire that he could apply to whatever goal or project he set his will toward.

But this challenge, a relationship with Katrina, was still an enigma to him. He grew defeated as hard work failed to pay off or move him forward or provide insights to future success. He didn't require perfection; just stability, just acceptance—but his practice of accommodation and generosity couldn't provide that. None of his investments in their marriage were reciprocated. He hadn't faced anything like this wall before. This resistance was not the dumb indifference of a game, or nature; it was calculated, cunning, recursive.

She chided him for his failure to repair bridges between them while quietly burning others during his constructive efforts, as if for the sole purpose of supplying fuel for ongoing derisions, so the problem could remain his fault, and she could remain righteous. David would have preferred a blind storm to this intentional wrenching of the works. His marriage was not a joint effort but a competition—not against circumstance, or the friction of carving out a living in the world, but a saboteur spouse. David's conscience, the informer of his willpower, was confused. He could not set his will against this nemesis as he did with life's other obstacles. He was trying to love the woman who demanded he build bridges for her to burn.

The endless conflict wasn't for any lack of bridges being built. David could talk about anything. He could find the common ground with anyone. But Katrina insisted on a void. She continually dug out new chasms between them, excavating common ground and charging David with bridging the gap.

David sought out sanctuary while I watched the kids but it was less clear to me what Katrina spent her evenings and weekends doing when her spousal workhorse wasn't available. I only asked about her plans a few times, just to make polite conversation, the more of which I could instigate the smoother our interactions went. But she routinely answered with a terse "errands." I learned to avoid that topic. I tried to be pleasant, although she made me feel uncomfortable. I never knew what might offend her or what conspiracy she might be dedicated to from day to day. There was an ever-present stress when Katrina was around. It was exhausting even in small doses. I understood why stability had become so valuable to my brother.

I knew that I needed Katrina to like me or at least consider me harmless in order to maintain an open door between David and me. If she preferred that he didn't see certain people, she had ways of achieving her agenda. She claimed a *de facto* jurisdiction over David's social life. Relationships outside her favor had a way of withering. She was the gatekeeper, the troll under the bridge. I had seen her trim out several of David's friends, even other siblings. I understood the necessity of playing buddy with her for a short second; then it was just the kids and me and we had a lot of fun together.

It was strange how few of the nights I babysat that David and Katrina went out together. Of course, with Katrina around, strange was becoming more common.

These ambiguous "errands" Katrina was always running came to mind when I heard about Katrina and Cain Perry. I had heard rumors—we all had—that she had been seen with him. People recognized him because he worked for the Perry County Sheriff's Department. He was City Marshall, meaning that he acted as the Sheriff whenever the elected Sheriff was unavailable or even just for the Sheriff's convenience.

I wasn't sure if I believed this rumor at first but the possibility of Katrina being less than faithful did not surprise me, although I expected her to be sneakier than this. Then it dawned on me that she wanted us to know. An affair was plausible, even likely, knowing what her and David's relationship was like.

In the beginning, Katrina had been immediately smitten with David who made good money for such a young man of twenty-one. He had worked in the oil fields in Oklahoma when they met. She wanted the financial security David could provide. She continued to relish David's good looks and as he made an effort to work out regularly she grew increasingly insecure. They looked like an unlikely pair—David, tall and muscular, Katrina, stumpy, like a shotgun shell packed with gunpowder.

Their relationship was asymmetrical. Katrina demanded so much and gave so little. David sacrificed so much and received so little support or comfort. There were very few displays of affection between them. Once in a while they exchanged a quick peck, and even then, it seemed motivated by a need to affirm a public image. She kissed him *because* there was an audience. Whenever this infrequently occurred, David's look of quiet surprise betrayed its rarity.

This was a telling difference from his first marriage. Theresa and David had always been touchy-feely, laughing and joking together. They made it no secret how they felt about each other. David always loved her and even after their divorce they remained great friends. It's a shame they were overwhelmed so young, but they did have a beautiful baby girl, Madeline.

I wondered if Katrina's rumored affair with Cain was her big plan to get revenge for David's "cheating." I suspected these rumors we kept encountering had something to do with those "errands" she was always so tight-lipped about. David didn't ask her about it. He didn't want to know. Perryville is a cozy community, what some might call a "cousiny" place, everybody knows everybody. Katrina knew this. I suspected this sloppiness was intentional, an accident with an aim. She wanted David to hear it. It was all part of the show.

I knew that Cain had a wife, though, and I doubted this visibility was part of his plan. With his large, pruned sideburns, and full-brim hat which he habitually took off and put back on, propping it at a cocky angle, Cain was not easy to confuse with anyone else. He was tall and skeletally thin. He carried himself with the gait of a Narcissus, sneaking glances of himself in shop window reflections and the mirror of his tinted Sheriff Department cruiser. He had the hooved swagger of a man that enjoys the sound of his boot heels clopping the pavement. Cain's reputation was an odd alloy of fear and ridicule. He held an allegiance to his own limitless liberties that gave him license to trespass on the freedoms of others in the name of public servitude.

While he was undoubtedly powerful and widely known to be unnecessarily cruel with the reigns of his position, he was also laughable, a walking caricature, a cartoon with a gun. He was arrogant in an almost pitiable way. His bravado veiled a nearly transparent schoolboy desire to be liked, or at least feared—classic bully psychology. After looking both ways, people shared stories of his intimidations and brutality, cases when it was only his word against another's. But in the same breath, they shared jokes deriding his vain tendencies and mirror-checking insecurity. Like an awkward teenager, he was positive he could be "cool" if he strove for such an image, yet this over-confidence was what made him a clown.

Several of David's friends had seen Cain and Katrina together on a few separate occasions. After much deliberation they finally decided to sit down with David and tell him what they had seen. David wouldn't hear it. He vehemently refused to believe what they told him. He was angry at them for telling him this. But it was true. And I believe David knew it was and wanted to ignore it to evade the rolling boil that such an accusation would surely ignite in Katrina. He preferred to deny the gross satisfaction she would get from his reaction. David had found some peace in this self-deception like the numb relief following extreme cold that signals hypothermia. She was so cold she burned, like dry ice, and her fire froze those in her path. Her arid eyes leeched tears from the eyes of others. Her false warmth, like a false spring, drew people to open up and bare their petals to her frost.

It was easier for David to look away. It was in his power to withhold the pleasure of this vindication. He wasn't there for Katrina, after all. He was there for his children. He knew he was trapped and was content to confine himself to the day-to-day duties of work and being a father. As for why David grew so irritated with some of his closest friends, saying things out loud can make them more real and more painful.

From Katrina's point of view, this was a fair and just battle to get even. In this petty war, Katrina fired all the bullets and rationalized the firing by saying David shot first. Once again, she justified her aggression as self-defense, accusing the provoked of provoking her.

As verbally agile as she was, speaking in self-serving sophistries and forked-tongue doublespeak, Katrina lived in a maze of her own concrete delusions. At times, these illusions were a benefit to her performances because she came to believe her own fabrications. Her outlandish fictions came to replace her true memory.

Still, her method-acting sometimes backfired and turned on her. As her perfectly memorized lies bled seamlessly into her reality, she periodically confused her scripts. I saw glimpses of Katrina disoriented, masked even to herself, in a hall of her own mirrors. She was not anchored to any true self and lacked a single skin to feel comfortable in. These sightings of Katrina, harried between costumes and scenes, were rare and fleeting, but they revealed a manipulator vulnerable to her own machinations. Like a child intent on scaring others with ghost stories who becomes scared in the process, Katrina's deception had a double edge.

Her sole motivation was an indiscriminate and blind need to win. Like a gambling addict looking for any contest or chance to place a bet, Katrina sought competitions, real or imagined, to win.

In the absence of a recognized game, winning meant making my aunts feel uncomfortable for the pleasure of watching them scramble. Winning was deflating someone's self-esteem with an insidious comment. Winning was faking a pregnancy to secure an advantageous marriage to a successful young man. Winning was instigating conflict for sport. Winning was attracting the attention of one man in order to mock another. This emotional roulette was a game to her, an opportunity to build herself up and tear someone else down.

The chatter about Katrina's affair died down as the scandal went stale. David's friends and family saw it was easier for him if they ignored it. It wasn't our place to choose David's battles for him. As I watched Sawyer begin toddling around, I was reminded why David wanted stability. Life went on as normally as could be expected.

My parents took a leap of faith and opened a small business, a restaurant. As dedicated entrepreneurs, they trusted in hard work and fairness. They illustrated the work-ethic that David had grown to emulate. Everyone in town knew where to find Mom and Dad, working at their restaurant.

The pleasant hum of restaurant conversation hushed one afternoon when a regular customer ran inside to tell my parents that several police vehicles were in front of David's house. They were shocked. Dad left immediately and rushed over to David's house to find out what had happened.

When Dad arrived he was terrified to see a SWAT team piling into formation outside his son's home. There was also a state trooper. The only representative of local law-enforcement was the City Marshall that had been seen repeatedly with Katrina.

Dad tried to go inside but was held back.

"But that's my son's house!" he protested to no avail.

The SWAT leader refused to tell my Dad why they were there, only that they couldn't get David to come out. This troop of law enforcement had already secured the perimeter and had all of David's neighbors vacate their homes. Dad asked to go inside and get his son so they could figure out this miscommunication, but the officers still wouldn't allow him to enter. None of these officers knew David, so Dad understood why they didn't take his protests seriously. These officers had heard it all before. But Cain Perry knew who David was. Cain sat in his cruiser, checking his hair in his rearview mirror. He knew what was going on but sequestered himself in his car.

Dad didn't understand why the SWAT team needed David to come out, and why they wouldn't just raid the house if this was so serious. SWAT teams don't usually get suited up to knock on doors. Didn't they have a warrant?

Meanwhile, David was asleep on his couch, entirely unaware of the storm brewing outside his door. The SWAT leader finally told Dad they were waiting on Katrina to come home and get David to come out. Dad didn't understand why they would wait for Katrina when they could just let him go inside and get his son. He didn't understand why they wouldn't tell him what all this was about in the first place. If there was someone dangerous inside, which there wasn't, why put another person in harm's way? Why did a SWAT team need someone else to open the door for them? None of this made sense, not then, not now.

After a few minutes, Katrina arrived. She ran past Dad without a word and spoke quickly with the SWAT leader before walking toward the house. She glanced back toward Cain's car as she walked up the stairs and went inside. She roused David and told him he needed to go outside but said nothing to prepare him for what he would find upon exiting his home.

Interestingly, she had him walk out first. He found an arsenal of assault rifles pointed at him. David froze, petrified, paralyzed, like a dream in which you cannot run. He had woken up in a nightmare. Slowly, but as fast as he could, he raised his hands, trembling, above his head. Then Katrina stepped out from behind him and began telling all these armed men that they had the wrong guy.

My uneasy brother began providing every available form of identification to prove to the officers that he was not the man they were looking for.

Come to find out, Chickasha law enforcement had received a tip from a woman in Perryville, Arkansas claiming that David Jay Brown, a fugitive from Oklahoma who was wanted for murder, was living in this house in Perryville. My brother's full name is Arvel David Brown. Cain Perry, who was present that day, knew that our David was no fugitive, yet he allowed the operation to proceed.

These two David's were dissimilar in everything but their names. This was a confusion that Cain Perry should have been able to clear up. The true fugitive was much shorter than my brother, and differed significantly in age. They looked nothing alike. If the law enforcement involved had bothered to investigate the tip before suiting up for battle, they would have discovered many discrepancies between the wanted murderer and my brother.

The entire operation was completely unconventional and incredibly sloppy. I am confident that Katrina had hoped it would have gone sloppier. If my brother had run off scared or back inside the house, as someone might do in such a blood-curdling situation, he could have been shot by some trigger-happy officer that had been told the man in his sights was a murderer.

The concert of coincidences was too unlikely to be taken as pure chance—a lady from Perryville called

Chickasha, where Katrina had lived and worked as a police dispatcher, where her family still lived. The SWAT team wouldn't allow my Dad to enter or even tell him why they were there but waited for Katrina to arrive, while Katrina's not-so-secret lover was present and did nothing to avoid this disaster of potentially lethal miscommunication.

I was in ninth grade. When I got home, I was immediately aware of the strange silence in our normally boisterous house. My brother was over. Everyone stared at me. Dad turned to David and said, "Well, you better tell her what happened."

I might not have even believed the ridiculous story if I didn't see how obviously shaken my sturdy big brother was. I was angry no one had thought to come get me from school. I was positive I could have explained everything. I could have done *something*.

In the weeks afterward, David's mailbox was stuffed with solicitous letters from attorneys in Arkansas and Oklahoma urging him to sue and choose them as his legal counsel. The case would be easy to win; no wonder it was attractive to litigators. News stations called him from both states hoping for an interview about the botched fiasco. It was sensational, ripe for a 6:00 o'clock special.

But David refused. That wasn't his style. He didn't care for that ambulance-chasing sensationalism even with the prospect of claiming a large sum of money. He found it petty even though he had been wrongly intimidated. To David, it was an honest mistake. Once again, his clear-headed desire to stay above the fray impressed me. His character was in a league of its own. He gave the world the benefit of a doubt. People, in general, were more good than bad, he felt.

But Katrina was angry at David for "wasting this opportunity" to sue or garner his fifteen minute fame doing interviews in Oklahoma and Arkansas. David didn't budge on his decision to abstain. It went against the grain of his character and personality. He didn't want to contribute to the greater problem he perceived in society, parasitic opportunism, a begrudged culture. Of course it had terrified him, it irritated him, but he felt it was just a ridiculous mistake.

"Truth is stranger than fiction," he had said when I had first heard the story after school that day.

"People just make mistakes, nobody is perfect," he told me.

He was at peace with the fact that this inevitable flaw was a part of human nature, part of the fabric of society. He had a pay-it-forward mentality. He knew that he too was capable of mistakes and he could only hope that when he blundered despite the best of intentions that people might forgive him as he had forgiven others. He made the argument that nobody gives law enforcement half as much attention when they do their job well as when they make a mistake. Such a scary mistake needed to teach those involved how to make sure it never happened again, but it wasn't deserving of slandering interviews or a profiteering lawsuit.

I suspected this incident hadn't been such an honest mistake. As a young girl, I lacked the wherewithal to voice such a controversial suspicion, but I possessed the maturity to realize it was better I not make any claim without evidence. I was perfectly aware what the collateral damage might be. I kept my eyes and ears open and my mouth shut. Years later, though, I discovered I wasn't the only one who had been suspicious, but resigned myself to further observation.

Chapter 7

Sawyer was now four-years-old, and no longer a baby. He could tell you that himself if you asked. I was looking forward to seeing him and his sisters that evening while David and Katrina were out.

As I walked up the steps of their house, I could hear one of the children crying inside. The cry quickened my step. Outside the front door, I could hear it was Sawyer. The girls, Lindsey and Madeline, let me in and I followed the cries to a room where Katrina was holding Sawyer.

She greeted me politely and began chatting nonchalantly about her day as her son bawled. She was unconcerned, as if calmly refusing to dignify a tantrum, so I thought perhaps Sawyer was throwing a fit as even the best children do periodically. But his wail never let up. His breathless cringing pitch made me hurt for him. He cried so hard for so long that his hot red face became, intermittently, silent in a muted scream, just long enough for his lungs to refill for the next wail. He was clearly in pain. The contrast between his pained face and Katrina's repose was unsettling. She smiled without radiance—her makeup, flawless as a painted mask.

Sawyer began moaning, "My shoulder hurts, my shoulder hurts," between his gasping sobs.

Katrina didn't seem to hear him. She kept talking, loud enough to project her voice over Sawyer's crying, but with a congenial tone, eerily aloof, as if trying to distract me. This was how her calculated charm entrapped people, with almost hypnotic detachment.

I interrupted her large supply of small talk, asking "What's wrong with him? Is he okay?"

"He just fell and hurt his shoulder, but he'll be okay," she said, as if I was needlessly alarmed and just being dramatic.

But I could tell Sawyer was in serious pain. This had been going on far too long to be explained away as a child's hammed up rebellion or a benign fall. There was something Sawyer wanted to tell me. I could see it in his eyes, widening at me, pleading. But he couldn't tell me here, not in front of his mother.

"Katrina, maybe we should take him to the doctor. I don't mind taking him," I offered, hoping to expedite the process.

"Oh no, he'll be fine," Katrina refused.

She went on with her one-sided conversation recounting every trivial detail of her day. I was increasingly uncomfortable. Katrina tried to invite me into her monologue with, "You know what I mean?" and "Then guess what happened?" She kept spouting diversions.

My growing empathy for Sawyer was becoming unbearable. But he was her son. I couldn't just grab him and go. She cut off my attempts to comfort Sawyer by talking over me, as if I was compromising her parental authority.

Thankfully, David drove up ,home from work. His truck became visible through the room's windows. Katrina watched intently as David got out of his vehicle and began walking toward the house. She had noticed his arrival immediately, observing his homecoming in a practiced way. This was why she was sitting here staring out the window, I realized, to watch for him. I wondered how many of her episodes had begun with her waiting for him, watching through that window.

David would know what to do. As soon as he walked out of the window's view, toward the house, Katrina suddenly started crying, blubbering, large tears rolled down her face with a pace that nearly matched the tears of her son. She finally seemed to realize this was a problem that couldn't be ignored. She knew David would say something.

David noticed the crying as soon as he walked in the front door. I heard his footsteps pause as he listened, then he accelerated toward us. He entered the room and saw Sawyer, whose resilient screams hadn't slowed since I had arrived. I watched that all-consuming parental worry envelope David's face.

"What happened?" he asked sharply

"He fell and hurt his shoulder," Katrina pouted.

David scooped up Sawyer from her lap and said, "Let's take him to the doctor."

Katrina grabbed her keys and headed out the door, David following behind with Sawyer in his arms.

Ultimately, we found out Sawyer wasn't faking anything to get attention or overreacting to a simple fall. His shoulder was sprained, but perhaps not by a fall. Young children are commonly injured if they are yanked up too hard by their arms, their developing joints can't take such sudden wrenching force.

Katrina hadn't been concerned with me or her children seeing her out of costume but I had seen a glimpse of the alternate show she performed for David. I filed the strange evening in memory, adding this enigma to my growing collection of suspicions. It was another jagged puzzle piece.

Weeks later, I was driving home after meeting with a study group at a friend's house. It was around ten that night and there, on the side of the road, I saw irrefutable evidence of that adulterous rumor we had all been hearing.

Cain and Katrina walked together, arms around each other's' waists. I realized who they were as I passed and in my rearview mirror I saw Cain smack Katrina's rear. That absolved any theory that they might just be friends.

I knew that if Katrina was out running her "errands" at this hour and hadn't asked me to babysit, then it meant David was at home with his kids this very moment. Their home was no doubt a more peaceful place without Katrina. I imagined David playing with the kids, content to wholly deny his wife was cheating on him, content to stack building blocks on the living-room floor with Sawyer or order plastic entrees from a menu that Madeline and Lindsey had drawn in crayon to play restaurant.

Although I can't say I was surprised to see proof of Katrina's affair, I had hoped the rumor wasn't true. I hoped against all the evidence that this affair was a figment of gossip, because I knew it would be easier for David that way. I realized that I, too, harbored some denial of this affair. For his sake, I had wanted David to be right in his denial.

I was disgusted with Katrina and nervous that she had involved Cain in her vendetta. I thought directly of how Cain had made no effort to clear up the miscommunication that brought a SWAT team to point their guns at my brother. What David had insisted was an honest mistake of law enforcement was beginning to look less honest. Katrina must have called in the false tip in hopes of a lucrative lawsuit or in hopes of something more sinister, a slip of a trigger. Cain had clearly been briefed by Katrina beforehand, since he stayed in his car against his strutting nature. This was a big event for Cain to have to sit out.

Cain's advanced age was irrelevant to Katrina. He was no different from the other people that Katrina engineered relationships with. Katrina never built a bridge for the sake of a relationship; there was always another reason.

Now she had a law enforcement officer in her toolbox. She had already succeeded in getting him to passively assist her; how long would it take before she had him programmed to take actions on her behalf?

I cringed on my way home, considering if this was the end of her agenda for Cain, or only the beginning. I dreaded what emboldened risks she might take now.

I hoped that Katrina would soon satisfy her craving for this sick sort of competition. I wished that David could be rid of her. Maybe she would decide that she had won this game of her own construction. Maybe she would get bored with this fixed contest and divorce David. I am confident our family would have approved, even David, if he could be assured he would share custody of Sawyer.

Now I knew for sure, having seen Cain and Katrina together with my own eyes. David's friends had been right. But I couldn't tell David, not after watching him flatly deny it when his closest friends told him. I would get a very cold shoulder if I tried. I had already seen it happen with several people David loved and trusted, even our mother. He surely didn't want to hear it from me, and once again I couldn't risk creating a barrier between us. I knew I wouldn't see the kids nearly as often if I went that route. He certainly already knew anyway. He didn't need me to remind him of this calculated attack on his pride.

Katrina was on a crusade to right an imagined injustice. She strategized that two of her wrongs could make a right, as if two deceptions could create something genuine. And she pursued this with extreme self-righteousness.

I didn't understand. If she wanted something outside of her marriage, why did she forbid the divorce when she negotiated with David? Why would she use

Sawyer as leverage to retain David only to cheat on him shortly after? Why not peacefully separate and share custody of the child she didn't want anyway?

The answer is that this wasn't the game Katrina was playing. Winning was everything to her. She had to fabricate fantastic resistance in the world that was out to get her to feed her appetite. Her conspiratorial narrative provided her a purpose. She defined herself in reaction to this alternative reality; this polarized perception facilitated a game, it created the opportunity to assert dominance on a battlefield of her choosing.

Chapter 8

As another night of babysitting for David and Katrina came to a close I put the children to bed and rested in a chair watching the windows flicker with silent heat lightning as I waited for my brother or Katrina to return. It was getting late. I heard a car pull up, a door close. I expected this to be David because he usually came home first, so I was surprised when Katrina walked in. She asked me where David was, clearly expecting him to have been home before her. I told her he had gone to the gym to play ball and he hadn't come home yet. She was irritated that he wasn't back.

I began gathering my things to head home when she asked me in a surreptitiously friendly way, if she could borrow my car for a minute. She said something about an errand she had forgotten, how she had always liked my car, and that she was low on gas. This caught me off guard; she was never without a motive. Her toothache-sweetness signaled something sour. It occurred to me that she wanted to drive my car to the gym and check if David was there. She wanted my car so David wouldn't know it was her when she pulled up.

She would have found him at the gym just like I told her, but I didn't want to enable her conspiracies against my brother.

"Sorry, I have errands to run," I said.

She knew I didn't intend to explain anything further. Her wide acquisitive eyes narrowed at me.

"Night," she said, and stomped away.

Walking out to my car, I heard her rifling through drawers and clanking dishes as her children slept. She wanted me to know she was angry.

I hoped this wouldn't motivate her to manufacture any division between David and me. Taking a stand against Katrina was always risky. Although it was my habit to avoid conflicts with her, this was a risk I was willing to take. If I had to lose David for a few weeks to protect him, so be it. I would make that sacrifice. I couldn't allow myself to be manipulated. Such sheepish appeasements whittle away one's self-respect and would give her precedent for more of these requests. What might she ask for next? I refused to give momentum to her wrecking ball paranoia.

Katrina was interesting to me in an anthropological way, like a case study. This deceiver was paranoid of being deceived and was incredibly jealous. The irony struck me as I drove home watching strings of lightning unravel, illuminating billowing clouds across a bruised purple sky.

My brother-in-law Thomas was playing ball with David that night. They hadn't finished their game yet.

"Hey David," he asked, "Why don't you go on home? It's getting late. It's okay if you need to go."

This friendly suggestion reminded David of the storm waiting for him at home. It exhausted him.

"I just don't want to go home," he replied despondently.

As soon as he got home he knew Katrina would accost him about the unfinished cabinets. He was ahead of schedule on the project, but that didn't matter now because Katrina had boiled it down to one of her coddled conflicts.

Our church had just moved into a new building. The walls were bare. Our pastor asked if David would mind building a large cross and covenant frame to be hung on the walls. He was happy to do it and excited for this opportunity to contribute. David didn't bury his talents for safekeeping; he shared them. He knew it wouldn't take long.

Everyone knew that David had a gift for building things. He was both an artisan and an artist. He was handy and had a mind for the mechanics of things but also possessed an eye for composition that allowed him to apply his imagination as well. He had even won a drawing competition as a teenager for a portrait of the Marlboro Man and received a cash prize. As his youngest sister, I was both impressed and intimidated by his various strengths. David was a hard act to follow.

The structures of these two small projects, a cross and a frame, were very simple for a carpenter of his experience. He would easily have them finished in a weekend. They would take longer to stain than to build, but Katrina openly criticized David for the small delay in the construction of her cabinets. Until the cabinets were built and installed, Katrina took every awkward opportunity to bring up the topic.

David had no idea why such a small delay bothered her so much. She acted as if he had volunteered for the project to spite her, as if the pastor's request was a conspiracy to exclude her by design when, in reality, David had repeatedly tried to include her in his church community.

David enjoyed going to services when he could. It was a good way for him to keep in touch with friends and family. He was social, and joked that he'd "never met a stranger." He found fellowship rejuvenating. Katrina always refused to join him. He never pressured her, but she fiercely refused his invitations. She actually got mad at him for leaving her for those couple of hours on Sunday mornings. If she was so clingy, I didn't understand why she didn't go with him. Although his continued invitations were proof he didn't mind for her to accompany him, I think he was pleased that he had one social circle she didn't want access to, although he hated not being able to bring his children with him. At any mention of the possibility of David bringing them along, Katrina flew into a rage. She justified her outrage by arguing that her refusal was because David went to a Baptist church and her family was Church of Christ, although she didn't currently attend.

This was a recurring battle for him. There was never a full solution. His choice was perpetually the lesser of two evils and fueling her manic vengeance was forever the greater evil.

David finished his game of basketball that night and went home, but Katrina's game wasn't over.

Less than a week before we lost David, I was called to watch the kids for the evening. When I arrived, Katrina was combing Lindsey's hair harshly, as if raking leaves through tall grass. When she was finished brushing, Lindsey, relieved, slinked away. Sawyer walked in and sat between his mother and me. Katrina reached over to pick up her keys which were on the table near Sawyer. He automatically ducked and put his hands up, defensively, over his head.

Katrina was a harsh disciplinarian. Frequently, David would come home from work and she would tell him to go spank Sawyer. Strangely, it was always Sawyer that needed the spanking. To keep peace with Katrina, David would go to Sawyer's room where the little boy had been hiding among blocks and action figures, too scared to play with them. David would explain very quietly, "I'm going to clap my hands loudly. When you walk out of this room, pretend you got a whipping, okay?" These staged spankings became routine because of how often Katrina requested Sawyer be spanked. David found her punishments excessive but knew that if he continued to argue with her about it both he and Sawyer would suffer for it. This charade was the only way to keep the peace—a lesser of evils.

Katrina and David left the house in a rush, each going their separate way without saying much to me and even less to each other. Shortly after they left, Lindsey came up to me. She was nervous. She was eight or nine at the time. I asked her if she was okay. I was worried that the rough combing had hurt her. She fidgeted for a moment, gathering her words, clearly upset about something.

Finally, she asked, "Why did Daddy look yellow?"

"What do you mean?" I asked.

"He just kept getting up and looking at himself in the mirror."

I reassured her that there was nothing to be worried about. I decided to comfort her first and try to understand what she meant later.

"Adults sometimes worry too much about how they look," I joked.

Her smile returned. I knew how incredibly imaginative children can be. I suspected her imagination had gotten the best of her, the way fears and anxieties turn all of our imaginations against us sometimes with nightmares and worries.

The kids and I went outside and I watched the three of them run around the yard, enjoying the mild September air in the waning evening light. They had grown so much since I had begun watching them. Sawyer was already six-years-old. They chased and tagged each other and kicked up leaves in flurries. They made a game of trying to catch the wind-loosed leaves in their whimsical descents to the ground. The harder they tried to snatch the leaves from the air the quicker they fluttered out of reach.

Soon it was impossible to see the falling leaves in the wan dusk. When we came back inside the kids were hot from playing and told me they were thirsty. I opened the refrigerator to see what was available. I saw David's pitcher of sweet tea so I offered it to the kids but they staunchly refused.

"We can't drink Daddy's tea," they said. They explained that their Mom said they could never have any of that.

Evidently, their mother had put the fear of God in them. Sweet tea was a forbidden fruit, and it seemed silly how this selectively concerned mother felt so strongly about her children's sugar consumption. She ignored them when they screamed in pain, but sweet tea made her fear for their health. I doubted that she was so adamant for the sake of saving it for David. She didn't even save herself for David. Besides, I knew he didn't care if his kids drank some of his tea. This is the American South; it is sacrilegious to forbid such a cultural staple as sweet tea.

But the kids insisted they shouldn't have any. They knew better than to cross Katrina, even with their friendly aunt unwittingly offering them what had been forbidden. They clearly didn't want to have to answer for the missing tea when their mother noticed and they were positive she would notice.

Katrina returned first that night. I left without seeing David.

I ran into my brother-in-law Thomas the following day. He had gone fishing with David the day before. David fished all over the state. He had even recently won a boat in a tournament.

Thomas and I caught up for a moment and then Thomas lowered his voice a little. "Has David been doing alright? He almost fell out of the boat yesterday."

I asked him how David fell. I expected some funny description of how he got tangled up in a mess of fishing line or dropped his pole in the lake. Thomas paused at my question, considering the cause. This wasn't a funny story. He was confused and worried.

"His legs kept falling asleep. He stood up and lost his balance," Thomas explained, "said that his legs had been bothering him lately."

David would be gone within the week.

Chapter 9

David was gone instantly. There was no time for any smoothing of this transition, no time to mull any acceptance. This abrupt void in our family allowed no time to prepare our hearts and minds for what life might be like without him. The void tore sharply across the fabric of our family, of our lives, like an earthquake separating the earth beneath us. Either we trembled or the earth shook. He had been young and healthy and alive only a week before.

We had already laid David to rest. I kept pinching myself, hoping to wake up, but ultimately everything was too relentlessly vivid to be a dream. I was paralyzed by this rupture, but I could not be more awake.

The permanence of his absence could slip my mind in fleeting seconds because it happened in such a blinding flash. I could actually forget he was irrevocably gone for the very fact that I thought of him constantly, trying to keep him near. I might encounter a question about something and make a mental note to consult my big brother, as I always had, only to remember a second later that this once simple phone call would be as impossible as trying to take flight with flapping arms. The full reality sunk in slow and heavy—a phone call wasn't only impossible today; it would be impossible forever.

I might read an article in a magazine or come across some news that I knew David would want to hear about. And again, and again, I ran into this impossibility. I was not accustomed to this freshly slammed door. I dreaded what it meant to become familiar with it, that the details of my memory might evaporate over time. I had done everything in my power to keep my relationship with my brother open—always making myself available to watch the kids, even humoring Katrina. But nothing I could do would ever open this door. We all accept this finality in theory, but when this door is slammed in your home there should be some recourse, some appeal, some negotiation. When you've just lost someone you shared so much life with, there should be a short grace period in which this closed door ought to crack open—just to allow a farewell, just to tie up loose ends, to tell him how much you really loved him.

The hole that David left in our family yawned open even in trivial daily conversation, the very kind we all tried to make to create something normal, something soothingly inconsequential. But the wound of loss opened repeatedly as I got tangled between past and present tenses when describing anything remotely related to my brother—any of his things, or friends, or places he frequented, or stories he had told. I floundered for weeks in this limbo, and never stopped thinking of things to ask or stories to tell him, then I began to remember that he was gone.

Meanwhile, Katrina and my mother continued to work at the same company in Conway where Mom had helped Katrina apply for a job years before. Mom had done everything she could to ensure David and Katrina could build their family together. Katrina had been unemployed, and was believed to be pregnant. So much had changed since then. With Katrina's cancellation of the autopsy still fresh on everyone's minds, Mom may have regretted this workplace proximity, but she didn't say so; it wasn't her style. She believed in civility. Mom didn't bring up the cancelled autopsy. What was there to talk about now? Her son was gone and buried. Fortunately, their jobs differed quite a bit, so they only saw each other in passing and exchanged nods.

Their coworkers took up a collection after hearing of their mutual loss. Several employees came to my Mom to offer their condolences and say they were keeping her and her family in their prayers. Mom appreciated the kind gestures and sympathetic cards, but this public aspect of mourning was exhausting. Even in the most genuine and friendly instances, it was difficult to be in the middle of a workday, trying to lose yourself in your work, trying to hold yourself together as if everything was okay, trying to make it to the end of another day, only to be reminded by good people of the void left by a lost son. Parents aren't supposed to outlive their children. It felt wrong.

Mom didn't bring up the topic of her loss at work. It wasn't a conversation she wanted to have. There wasn't a decisive cause of death for her to disclose when curious people asked in their varyingly nuanced ways. And without a clear cause of death, a short exchange could drag on into well-meant but painful speculation.

Tragedy can be sensational to those with a view of the crash but unscathed by it. Mom began to hear chatter around the office that David had died of an aneurism. When she initially overheard this theory, she calmly explained that they didn't know what had caused David's death, but that it was very sudden, so she could understand why someone might leap to that assumption. Mom didn't think any more of it. People talk and speculate; she didn't begrudge them that. After all, her son's death was a mystery to her as well. But because it was a mystery, she couldn't allow such an assumption.

She felt she had put that rumor to rest, but as the weeks pressed on she continued to hear it and grew tired of repeatedly explaining that they didn't know what had taken David. She began asking where people had heard this aneurism theory, hoping to squelch this gossip. Every branch of that grapevine led to her daughter-in-law, Katrina.

While Mom was worn down by talking about David's death, Katrina was molding it into a juicy drama. No wonder the aneurism rumor had travelled so fast. People no doubt believed it since it had been spread by the wife of the deceased.

The truth was there wasn't a decisive explanation for David's death. The reality was more painful than Katrina's fiction. While Mom felt it important to prevent false guesses from taking root,

Katrina was intent on getting the first word. The single word "aneurism" would do because it could be summed up easily, no difficult explanation of unknowns. She wanted others to talk about it so that she wouldn't be confronted with the mystery. She didn't want to be asked questions, so she spread her alternate ending freely, planting the seeds of a lascivious vine. It was a diversion, and the best way to divert the curious from the mystery was to supply an answer, something sensational they would be inclined to share further.

Katrina's lie spread like wildfire. Mom, fatigued as she was, did her best to put out these flames. She needed people to understand that it was yet to be determined what had caused her son's death. She wondered if she might ever know. Mom deduced Katrina's motivation for spreading this rumor was a mix of her typical lust for attention as well as a new fear that if people understood the true circumstances of David's death they might find it conspicuous that Katrina had somehow averted an autopsy desired by the family and mandated by State Law.

The workplace collection was divided into thirds: two-thirds for Katrina, one-third for Mom. Mom didn't mind. What could money do? No amount of petty cash could return David to her. It was painfully ironic, though, that Katrina should receive the largest donation from these wholly well-intentioned people who assumed she had large funeral expenses when, in fact, Katrina had refused to pay for any part of the funeral even as she made claims on several insurance policies set up by David to cover things like funeral expenses.

My parents paid for all of it after they were embarrassed by a call from the funeral home about nonpayment. They tried to get Katrina to help with the expenses by only buying the headstone, but she failed to purchase one and after a few weeks Mom could no longer allow her son's grave to go unmarked. So my parents gave in and purchased the headstone as well.

Mom didn't want to compete in Katrina's drama. She paid no mind to her smug stares at work. Mom knew that Katrina looked for the slightest spark of conflict to fan into flames. But Mom denied her that kindling; she avoided conflict with Katrina because it would only fuel her and exhaust our family. Besides, Mom knew that no petty victory over this frenetic instigator could alleviate what caused her pain. She only needed to stay close enough to Katrina to make sure her grandbabies were taken care of. Mom was well aware that Katrina might cut her out of their lives. Mom was worried about Sawyer and Lindsey. We all were.

With David out of the picture, Katrina had no further script to play nice with the kids. I reflected on the behavior she had tailored for David, putting on the mask of an earnest mother. It came on and off with the flip of a switch. It was as if she had been playing house for those seven years they had been together.

She was cold toward Sawyer, as she was toward Madeline, but Madeline had her biological mother to lean on after Katrina's emotional lacerations. I worried about Sawyer, no less alone, being with his mother. She told him and Lindsey that Madeline was no longer their sister and refused to answer their questions. She offered no explanation for how their lives were changing during this traumatic loss. While David wasn't Lindsey's biological father, she had been led to believe that he was. David had always been Daddy to her so her loss was no less painful. I wondered if Katrina now regretted installing that program in her daughter's mind.

With all of David's belongings boxed up or gone from their home, along with Madeline, Sawyer's strong resemblance to David was Katrina's only reminder of her deceased husband. Madeline had Theresa. Lindsey had Katrina. But I worried for Sawyer, caught in the middle. I hurt for him.

Immediately after his father's untimely and wholly unexplained death, Katrina began purging their house of David's things. She seemed just as happy to be rid of Madeline as she was to clear out closets of David's belongings.

Katrina had helped raise Madeline for seven years of her life, but she felt no connection to her anymore. It had always been transparent that Lindsey was Katrina's favorite. She was dealt lighter punishments and allowed more choice and autonomy than either Sawyer or Madeline. Surprisingly, the three of them got along very well with each other.

Katrina's favoritism created unique problems for Lindsey because her special treatment was obvious to her siblings. Yet Sawyer and Madeline understood that it was beyond Lindsey's control, and they perceived how conflicted Lindsey felt about it. They saw that she felt guilty about something she had no control over. This unfair treatment was as shamefully awkward for Lindsey as it was volatile and shunning for Madeline and Sawyer.

Outside of Katrina's immediate supervision, the children shared a bond in spite of Katrina's divisive parenting. Children can be so wise.

I tried to understand Katrina's peculiar purging of everything related to David. Was this icy behavior a coping strategy, a way for her to deceive, to insulate a delusion of invulnerability by discarding all triggers of his memory? Or was she really this cool and collected to accept such random tragedy as a natural course of events.

I had the opposite problem. I knew I couldn't keep everything, but I tried to for a while. A ticket stub from a movie David and I had seen together was invaluable when I found it in a drawer. It is common for people who have lost a loved one to have a difficult time realizing they should not keep every little thing.

Katrina carried out box after box.

The only tears I had seen fall from her eyes through this entire waking nightmare had been for an empty casket at the funeral home as we made arrangements. And now I wondered if that breakdown had been a tearful ruse to skip out on a chore and avoid setting up a payment plan.

Whenever people in the community or at work asked how she was doing or if she needed anything, she continued to say that she "just wanted it all to be over."

Katrina employed that phrase to cut conversations short. It was the same argument she had used that awful night in the hospital as she fought with my heartbroken parents and the rest of our family attempting to deny the autopsy.

David had a rent-house a few blocks away from their home. The rental property was already bought and paid for, free and clear. David had saved to purchase the fixer-upper and had done a lot of remodeling in order to rent it. It was an investment he intended to use to help support his children later in their lives.

The same week of David's funeral we noticed a sign in front of the rental house. Katrina was selling it. One of my sisters asked a friend to call and pretend to be interested, to find out the selling price. The asking price was a measly $23,000, a liquidation steal of a price for that lucky buyer. She may have even sold it cheaper than the asking price. Katrina wasn't concerned with getting an investment back out of the property; it was all profit to her.

Katrina told my brother Robert that he should come get the large collection of tools David had accumulated over the course of all his projects, as well as the prize fishing boat David had won. Robert drove into town to get his brother's dearest things, mementos of the years they spent working and playing together. Katrina, however, acted surprised when he showed up, like she wasn't expecting him despite having specifically requested he retrieve these things. She had already given them away to one of her friend's husbands.

Katrina's explanation was "I forgot."

Robert was both furious and crushed. In shock, he came over to my parent's house. Angry despair dampened his face. I had seen this peculiar mix of heat and sadness before in my Dad's face the night we lost David.

Chapter 10

A few weeks after the funeral, Theresa and Madeline came from Chickasha, where they now lived, to visit us at my parent's house in Perryville. We couldn't allow Madeline to think the loss of her father had cut her off from the rest of us despite Katrina's effort to marginalize her from her siblings.

Madeline asked me if she could go get one of her father's hats from Katrina. David had always worn baseball caps and his daughter wanted one to remember him. I was moved by her earnest request, and I offered to drive her over to pick a hat. I usually did what I could to avoid Katrina, but I expected this to be a simple errand. An old hat didn't have the resale value of a rent-house or a fishing boat.

After seeing how motivated she was to put his memory behind her, I thought Katrina might be happy to give away some mementos. How was she so tough? I had once been impressed by what I thought was her strength but now knew it to be a hard, thin shell. I wasn't impressed by her ability to make light of the heavy in life. But perhaps, for once, her disaffection could benefit Madeline by making a keepsake available.

We knocked and Katrina came to the door. She didn't have any canned small-talk for us today. We greeted her and she nodded in silence, ready to get to the issue and move us along. That was fine with me. I had no intention of loitering among piles of my lost brother's belongings any longer than I needed.

I looked at Madeline, cuing her to make her humble request.

"Can I have one of his hats?" she asked.

Surrounded by boxes marked "trash," Katrina answered in a monotone far more unsettling than any growl; "No."

That single word knocked the air out of Madeline. We waited as a stale silence settled around us like wet snow. Was this another poorly timed jab that Katrina would soon label a "joke?" Was this another game to give her the satisfaction of watching us jump? She offered no further justification. She refused to dignify us with any explanation. She felt unabashedly superior now that my brother was gone.

I didn't know what to say when bold, young Madeline, only nine, looked up to me for some translation of this chilly confrontation. Without a word to offer her, she began to fall apart, spirit crushed, soul bruised. She pleaded between sobs, "Please, just one thing?"

Katrina stared a thousand yards through us—as if Madeline's weeping were an annoying car alarm or a squeaky wheeled cart at the grocery store. What was this neurological glitch? Katrina was wired differently.

I couldn't take another slow second of this soulless stunt. Katrina stared down her sharp nose, condescending and detached. Her eyes had the shallow glint of marbles, opaque and refractive, thin surfaces hiding the emptiness behind them. Her crowded features sunk toward the middle of her face. I took a step in the doorframe, intending to quickly grab a visible ball cap and end this glacial power play.

Katrina blocked my passage and smirked. I had seen that smirk before, outside the hospital. Once again, it sent a shiver down my spine. A surreal static hummed behind my ears. The hairs on my arms stood up.

She was entirely untethered from the suffering around her. She was an emotional torturer; morally vacant, ethically empty.

The pride in her face might have convinced someone who couldn't see or hear Madeline that Katrina was on a righteous crusade against some powerful aggressor rather than a heartbroken little girl. No perceived foe was too small for Katrina's scorched-earth tactics.

I grabbed Madeline and we left. I told her I probably had something of David's at home that she could have. We were both exhausted by this confrontation. Katrina hadn't flinched. She never blinked. There was no sign that this child's pleading had tugged any heartstrings. Perhaps her strings were tied to something other than a heart.

I realized that this indomitable indifference was a subspecies of evil. Evil is not always hot violent fury. Her mode of destruction was often stoic, apathetic, and emotionally negligent. This was not passionate, fiery, theatrical violence, but this calculated infliction was definitely inhuman. I don't believe anything could have hurt Madeline more than Katrina's unmoving silence. It was psychologically devastating to be unheard, as if unable to scream in this bad dream. Katrina's strategic detachment had a mirroring effect, making those around her feel estranged.

Her refrigerated remorselessness reminded me of Dante's ninth level of hell, the home of traitors and fraudsters and Satan, buried to the waist in ice, eternally flapping his wings, whipping a wind that only freezes him further. There was a hell inside Katrina that her flapping froze over.

Her inanimate emotion was making her an "It" to me, as it was clear we were to her. This objectification made her even scarier. She wasn't playing the game of life by the same rules. She was invulnerable to the trappings of love and conscience, those human connections that give life its color, yet make us susceptible to heartbreak and loss. Her world was populated with dumb, expendable action figures, pathetically encumbered with the handicap of a conscience.

Not long after that standoff, Katrina discovered Madeline *would* be getting something of her father's after all—not a hat, but an insurance payout. Katrina was informed she was not the sole beneficiary. Her ballistic temper erupted in a predictable rage.

She was so furious she went to the human resources office at David's former workplace and did her best to bully the two ladies that were working there that day, trying to pressure them to change David's designations in the insurance paperwork. These ladies didn't have the power to change David's arrangements even if they had wanted to. They tried to explain this to Katrina. Making such a change would be tantamount to altering a deceased person's last will and testament. The notion was sacrilegious and it was obviously illegal. But Katrina wouldn't listen to this logic. Like throwing water on a grease fire, efforts to calm Katrina only caused her to flare even more.

Her hysteria might have led someone to believe she had been cut out entirely, that she wouldn't receive anything, but that was hardly the case. She would still get a hefty lump sum. The individual she was so outraged to share a portion of her new fortune with was a nine-year-old girl.

Katrina finally left the H.R. office. After witnessing such belligerence, the ladies feared what Katrina might do in her rampage. They called our home to warn my parents. Katrina had made some threats regarding Madeline. Some of Katrina's harsh words were too revolting to repeat, the ladies told my mother. The fact that they refused to repeat them spoke volumes.

My mother hung up the phone with a sour face of gut-knotting dread just as Katrina burst into our home without a knock. She had come straight over.

"Your son is a liar! He lied to me!" she yelled at my parents. She was hysterical. My impulse to run for cover was staid by my shocked curiosity. Why would she do this? What could she possibly accomplish by cursing our lost loved one?

To prove to us that David was a liar Katrina told us how she had asked him if she was his sole beneficiary. But she had just found out that she wasn't, therefore David had been a liar.

This, of course, was a conspicuous question for Katrina to have asked David. I could tell she realized she had slipped up because she paused in her tantrum for a second before careening on to kill the silence. I filed away this strange disclosure in case it proved useful. Why and when did Katrina ask David if she was his sole beneficiary?

I realized Katrina wasn't looking for sympathy in this scene of her drama. She wasn't the martyr of this performance; she was the alpha. She was attempting to bully my parents into doing something about it. She foolishly assumed they could.

My parents were cautious of Katrina; they never knew what she might be capable of in a rage like this. She had been jealous of Madeline from the very beginning. David's focus on his daughter was what had led him to breakup with Katrina the first time. Katrina considered his paternal devotion to Madeline a threat. This early jealousy was inflamed by David's reluctance to formally adopt Katrina's daughter Lindsey. David didn't expect Katrina to adopt Madeline either.

Katrina did her best to squelch and wither David's relationship with his daughter in subtle and calculated ways. With persistent little sabotages she was always testing David to see how far she could go before he would decide he'd had enough and that it was worth it to him to confront her and invite the inevitable fight to follow. She would make him late to visit Madeline, and engineer scheduling conflicts with David's shared custody schedule. After this surprise deduction from her insurance windfall, Katrina now felt even more righteous in her irrational grudge against this little girl.

Now, listening to her hissing derisions of my recently deceased brother and my grieving young niece, I remembered that snarl I had seen the day we first met Katrina. This was her raw character, her true unmasked face. She had no need to perform now with David gone.

She had been so calm and collected on family night and so together during the funeral while we were all addled and shattered. Yet here she was in a fever over insurance—green with envy before the flowers had wilted at his resting place. I had never seen her so angry, and I had seen her seething on numerous occasions.

Later on, as I began compiling paperwork in search of some explanation for my brother's abrupt death, I found that David had changed his beneficiaries shortly before his death. I imagine he was confident that Sawyer would be taken care of by his mother. David's specific designation of Madeline tells me that he was worried she might get the short end of the stick if Katrina was the delegator of funds. I am so proud of David for doing that. What tremendous forethought for a twenty-eight-year-old to make that change for his daughter's sake. How could he have expected those changes to be utilized only three months later? But then again, I worry that he did have such a suspicion.

Something inspired him to make that change; maybe the fact that she asked him if she was the sole beneficiary. Death is something we must all plan for in order to spare our families added stress and financial turmoil. It doesn't surprise me that David considered these details. What surprised me was the timing of this adjustment to his insurance plan.

After that discovery, I took it upon myself to further review his insurance plan since the details of it were igniting such nasty disputes. I soon discovered that the plan wouldn't payout the full amount unless they had been married for more than seven years.

Had it been seven years? Was Katrina about to find yet another money-shrinking surprise? I wondered if we should expect another greedy tirade from her, so I calculated how long they had been married.

At the time of David's death, they had been married seven years and three months. Interestingly, this placed Katrina's tactless question about being David's sole beneficiary near the time of their seventh anniversary and just three months before his death. The timing was conspicuous.

After Katrina's latest rampage, she left town to visit her family in Chickasha. We were relieved to be rid of her for the time being.

Days later we heard from Madeline's mother. Theresa still lived in Chickasha. She had taken Madeline shopping that day. When they stepped off the sidewalk to walk out to their vehicle in the parking lot a truck pulled out and accelerated toward them. Theresa broke into a sprint and shoved Madeline to get them both out of the way. It never even slowed and continued accelerating out of sight.

Both Theresa and Madeline recognized the truck. It was the new vehicle Katrina had already purchased with the insurance money. They knew it was her, without a doubt, because of the tacky bumper sticker Katrina had put on it. The sticker, which was popular with teenagers at the time, read "Ain't Skeered." That juvenile and typically benign, if brash, phrase was pregnant with nefarious double meaning to our family and we knew this alternate reading was not lost on Katrina. This was characteristic of her taunting style, enough bite to hurt, enough ambiguity to allow for her retreat, enough room to be outraged by anyone's outrage. She could accuse any critic of seeing something that wasn't there. She engineered provocations that would give her the opportunity to play dumb. She courted the game.

Theresa filed a report with the Chickasha Police Department where Katrina had previously worked as a dispatcher. It could have been chance that Katrina happened to visit Chickasha just after her realization that she would have to share the money with Madeline, whom she knew would be in Chickasha with her mother. It could have been chance that she happened to see them out shopping. Chickasha is not a large place. But it wouldn't surprise me if Katrina had followed them with that purpose in mind. The small size of Chickasha doesn't make it difficult to bump into people you know, accidentally or intentionally. What would Katrina have said if she had been successful in running them down? Or was her aim to taunt and intimidate?

Her volatility ceased to surprise me. These once anomalous aggressions were now a pattern of predictably unpredictable behavior.

A few days later, my Dad walked out on his front porch and found a package. It was a large envelope, a style that Katrina used regularly.

He opened it to find photographs of his deceased son lying in his casket. This was not a friendly sharing of photos. These weren't intended for a scrapbook. They weren't the type of pictures a parent would want to keep to help them remember. It was sick that she had taken these photos, sicker still that she cowardly left them for my Dad to find. Katrina was back in town.

A few months afterward, I was grocery shopping with my mother in Perryville. Through the course of our shopping I kept noticing a woman staring at us. After having already caught her staring a few times, she wound up on the same aisle as us. She pretended to browse the shelves while clearly watching us. It wasn't just me. I had almost hoped it was a misperception, like I had hoped Katrina's snarl at Madeline was a figment. But it was real. This was creepy.

I tugged my Mom to another aisle and explained what had made me uncomfortable. As I whispered my explanation, the same woman peeked around the corner at the far end of the aisle. I insisted we leave. We hurried through the checkout and rushed to load our groceries into the car.

That woman came up beside me in the parking lot. I jumped. She introduced herself, first name only.

"I'm a doctor, a psychiatrist," she said.

She turned to my Mom. "Are you David's mother?"

"Yes..." she answered, unsure of where this was going.

"I am sorry for staring," she apologized. "I could lose my job over this, but I need to tell you that your daughter-in-law is not well.

She explained that Katrina had episodes. She was incapable of the feelings most of us experience. The anonymous doctor explained that Katrina was either born that way or it was a learned behavior. I remembered that Katrina's father died suddenly at a young age, just like David.

Katrina was described as being uninhibited by what we call a conscience. It seemed this condition was what most people would describe as sociopathic.

We prefer to think that these people don't exist, that they don't sit next to us in traffic, or work in our offices, or trick our brothers into marriages. Their existence is difficult to acknowledge because it puts a face on what we tend to call evil. And the face is more unsettling when it doesn't fit our concept of what evil looks like. Evil can look like anyone.

"Please look into your son's death. Don't give up," the doctor said.

And that was it. The doctor walked off into the shadows.

I doubted David had known the full extent of Katrina's condition. He had mentioned before that it was important she remember to take her prescription for a chemical imbalance. Maybe this was why he was able to blow off so many of her tantrums and schemes. He wrote them off as symptoms of a peculiar sadness. He had always been accommodating. He made extreme allowances. David didn't talk about it beyond mentioning the importance of her taking her pills regularly. I seriously doubt he realized she was being treated for a range of personality disorders.

Who knows what Katrina had told that doctor or other doctors that couldn't be formally accessed due to patient confidentiality. Those files were locked out of reach. Still, I did learn of something called "duty to warn." It's one of the few exceptions to patient confidentiality. It requires that clinical psychologists disclose when they have a reason to believe someone is in imminent danger, whether the potential victim is the patient, the psychologist or a third party. This information must be supplied to the person in danger or law enforcement.

This doctor clearly felt that foul play was possible, but had been conflicted about whether to breech patient confidentiality. The doctor would have had to prove that they had reasonable cause to believe danger was imminent to retain her license in the event that Katrina contested. Such a risk could throw a career under the bus. Maybe this doctor was scared of Katrina too. Whatever the doctor had heard, it had been alarming enough to weigh on her conscience.

We began collecting David's medical records and the reports filed by Dr. Mallard and the two nurses from the night of his death. This effort led us to a string of conspicuous discoveries.

Katrina falsified the paperwork that she had filled out at the hospital before we arrived with Mom from Conway. She gave a false address and phone number and claimed she did not have insurance and selected "private-pay" rather than utilizing either her or David's insurance. Why would she elect to pay such an expense out of pocket?

Chapter 11

It was now almost six months since we had lost David. Each time I ventured outside, the dampness of March led me to wonder if I had just missed a light shower. The warming spring light and the sprigs of new green foliage suggested that renewal might be possible even if only in small ways.

Some of my brother's friends came up with a plan to take some gifts over for David's children and they kindly chose to include my parents and me. We all met at my parent's house with our wrapped presents, excited to see the look of surprise on their faces when we arrived.

We travelled a block over to Katrina's house. We knocked and Katrina let us in with a testy look on her face. She didn't say a word, as if she didn't want to get her voice dirty with a "Hello." She snorted and her nose pulled up as if retreating from her own breath. Beforehand, I had thought that not even Katrina could get upset about this since we were just bringing toys to her kids and leaving. But I was wrong.

Meanwhile, the refreshing look of surprise on Sawyer and Lindsey's face temporarily put me at ease. In awe, Sawyer asked if he could open the gift he had just been handed. Apparently this was the last straw for Katrina. Before we could say "Of course, gifts are for opening," she erupted, "No! What you and your sister can do is go to your rooms!"

As they skulked off, a heavy silence fell. This was awkward. I wasn't sure whether to leave without a word, or ask what the problem was, or apologize, as ridiculous as that would have been. My brother's friends and my parents and I looked at each other wondering what might happen next. None of us had expected Katrina's fireworks in this situation. This had been intended as some sort of olive branch, a reminder that we were still family.

Katrina turned back to us with a strange smile. The features of her face scrunched, sinking inward, like water down a drain.

"And ya'll need to leave," she said, scanning each of us. "You're not welcome here."

This guiltless personality, so comfortable in its own skin, had the paradoxical ability to make others uncomfortable in their own. My stalwart mother's eyes burned with quiet heat. My father's fist tightened into a gavel that shook with titanic tremors. I knew this type of stress wasn't good for his heart. Dad stood up to shepherd us out of that house, but one of David's friends couldn't hold back any longer.

"You're only hurting those kids," he said.

After hearing that, Katrina herded us out, cursing each of us. She followed my Dad to the vehicle, and slammed the car door on him before he could get in his seat. She slammed a door on an elderly man who was already battling significant health issues and was more depressed than he could tell anyone.

Now that my parents realized how difficult it would be to stay in contact with their grandson, they chose to go to court for grandparent's rights. They had hoped to be able to see Lindsey as well, but legally they could only pursue visitations with Sawyer, because Lindsey was technically their step-granddaughter. This legal detail crushed my parents. They had always considered Lindsey their granddaughter; Lindsey had always considered them her grandparents. We knew that Katrina had never told Lindsey that David wasn't her biological father. We feared what explanation, if any, Katrina would give Lindsey if she asked why she couldn't go to grandma and grandpa's house along with Sawyer. We feared Katrina's typically divisive tactics; we feared she might tell Lindsey that we didn't want to see her, that she might present this as contrived evidence that we weren't still a part of Lindsey's family.

The judge granted my parents visitation every other weekend. Twice my mother went over to pick up Sawyer. Katrina was actually supposed to deliver Sawyer to my parent's house, but my mother wanted to see him too much to be impeded by Katrina's petty refusal to drive him, so Mom went herself. It was heart-wrenching for my mother to hear Lindsey begging Katrina to go with Sawyer. But there was no legal recourse to allow Lindsey to go.

Lindsey had the dubious honor of being Katrina's favorite, but those special privileges were useless in this situation. Katrina was impassive. It was incredibly hard for my Mom and Sawyer to leave

Lindsey behind. The injustice haunted my Mom. She kept contacting lawyers, trying to find a way to see Lindsey.

When Mom brought Sawyer home for the first visitation he played with building blocks, and little cars with all the seriousness of a civil engineer. Then he jumped up, as if he had just remembered something important.

"Oh, and Mom told me to tell you thanks for buying Daddy's headstone because you saved her some money."

Katrina drafted her children to puppet snide jabs. There was something sinister in hearing her voice through her children. She sent Sawyer with an incendiary statement, and hid behind him. Sawyer was innocently unaware of the ill-intent behind this message. He had been led to believe it was a grown-up joke that he didn't understand, but he laughed, pretending to understand. When in doubt, we tend to mimic our elders. But here at his grandma's house, all the adults were just as confused by this "joke" as Sawyer was. Relieved, he returned to playing, like a messenger finally free of his burden.

Every subsequent visitation weekend after the first two, my Mom went over to Katrina's house and attempted to pick up Sawyer. Month after month, Mom repeatedly went over and knocked, all the while hearing Katrina inside telling the kids to be quiet, pretending they weren't there. My Mom recognized this ruse, of course, but she kept going over and trying all the same.

138

It was important to Mom not to allow Katrina to think she had given up. She wouldn't give up. She planned to go back to court as soon as she could because of Katrina's refusal to acknowledge the court-ordered visitations.

We made the decision to employ professional investigators to help us find answers about the missing hospital payments. After seeing the paperwork that Katrina had falsified, we were curious what else she may have tampered with. This effort proved to be more of an adventure than we expected.

The first P.I. came from Little Rock to meet with my parents. Before they could explain anything, the detective said "If you want her to be guilty, she'll be guilty for $5000."

At first I thought *Yes! Finally! Swift short-order justice served!* But Mom was appropriately appalled.

"No, we can't have that on our conscience. Right is on our side. There's nothing to be gained in muddying that."

Mom preferred that justice be served cold, if it had to, rather than microwaved. This sort of thing wasn't supposed to happen in America. Bribery and blackmail were supposed to be ailments of less developed societies. This man was no snake oil salesman. He was well known. He had binders full of investigative work. He was experienced. But how many times had he made this offer before, without a moral compass?

The investigator wasn't even embarrassed by my Mom's refusal. It was just the course of business for him. He politely wished us a good evening and left like a travelling salesman, numb to rejection and faithful to his quota. He was unfazed, but we were shaken. If a conviction cost $5000, what was the price of innocence for an affluent criminal?

Had we taken that candy-coated offer we would've been contributing to the same flawed system we were struggling against. We could not make cogs of ourselves and appease this machine for selfish gain. We would confront this honorably in the light of day. We believed that for our justice system to function properly, everyone must play by the same rules, although it was becoming clear that everyone didn't share this ideal. The reality was murkier—polluted by greed and power.

Maybe this P.I. didn't actually have the means to deliver on this offer, maybe it was a con. If we had paid him and it didn't come through, what recourse would we have without incriminating ourselves? This was unsavory from every angle. Obviously, we did not choose to work with this man. Interestingly, we later discovered he was working out of the office of a lawyer that had been incriminated in Gene Wirges' book, *Conflict of Interests,* a detailed investigation into the machine politics that permeated neighboring Conway County during the 1960s under High Sheriff Marlin Hawkins. This lawyer later lost his license for reasons that were never fully explained.

Eventually we were introduced to some very capable and amiable investigators. They explained that a private-pay selection on Katrina's paperwork was likely chosen to avoid drawing the attention of insurance companies. For some reason, she didn't want a team of insurance lawyers meddling. It *is* quite strange for a twenty-eight-year-old with no history of health problems to die so unexpectedly and not have an autopsy.

We still don't know how the hospital bill was paid or who paid for it. The hospital didn't have that information. They thought they did, but when that information was requested, they apologized for not being able to find it. There is no paper trail. They have no record of billing or payment, no history of the transaction, as if it never happened.

While searching through David's medical records, I was reminded of a simple sinus surgery he had about six months before his death. The doctor's notes detailed how healthy he was and how rapidly he recuperated.

Young men who recuperate rapidly don't typically die suddenly of natural causes. There was a missing link here. The body of evidence we were compiling was becoming alarmingly consistent. We were beginning to see an incriminating pattern of manipulation and deception. Individually, these instances might be written off as mistakes or denials, but in concert, they formed a pattern that suggested foul play. These consistent inconsistencies begged further inquiry.

The investigation pressed on. We waded through bureaucratic barriers in search of any information that might shed light on my brother's death. My father was exhausted by this tumult and saw increasing evidence to validate the initial gut feeling he had that night in the car, driving to get Mom.

"She did it. She finally did it," he had said.

Dad passed away in November 1995, about a year after he had lost his son. It was a year bookended with loss for our family. Following the second death in our family in roughly a year, I was swimming in tragedy, and fatigued from trying to keep my head above water. At twenty-two, I was beginning to suspect that the loss of loved ones was a hallmark of adulthood. At an age when many of my peers were seeking out new frontiers, I craved conclusion and normalcy. It was a struggle like nothing I had ever faced—a grueling marathon without a finish line.

I survived by focusing on simple things and staying busy with dutiful to-do lists. Pressing forward by setting my mind to tasks helped me avoid wandering into entrapping memories and ruts of despair. I had to keep moving. Everything in my life was so open ended, yet confining. My equation for the future was frozen by too many variables and unknowns. There was no constant. Alongside the youthful possibility of the world before me, was the undeniable reality of closed doors to two of the dearest people in my life. Amid such dizzying chaos, trivial errands or washing the dishes became therapeutic. There was relief in routines.

I applied and got a job working in the physical and occupational therapy department at the hospital in Morrilton. At first, it was very uncomfortable being so close to that room where I'd seen David's body. But it was a good job and I needed it. I grew numb to the reminders of tragedy after a few weeks. I suspect that skin-thickening was a subconscious desire. I wanted to prove to myself that I could do it. If I flooded myself with what I feared most then maybe I could assimilate this void into my life. I dove into my job at the hospital like jumping into the shower with a sunburn, all at once, just to get the sting over. Still, some days that sunburn blistered and peeled.

Now that I was spending so much time at the hospital, I was struck by the irony of how many health professionals never missed a smoke break. Watching the nurses outside, conversing between exhalations, I recalled the sight of Katrina smoking nonchalantly by that same hospital sign, flicking the ash, in her affected manner. I remembered the false hope that the sight of her casually smoking had given me.

"He's gone," she'd said with an intellectual detachment—like it was a theoretical problem.

I thought I would be okay if I just kept pressing forward, if I refused to allow this persistent weight to anchor me in a hole. Stagnancy would trap me. I had to keep moving, fast enough to dodge the raindrops.

Driving through Perryville, running some errand, I was forced to come to a stop. There must have been a wreck or roadwork because traffic was backed up.

And who should happen to pull up on my right after pulling out of the Farm Bureau Insurance parking lot but Katrina in that same new truck she had charged at Madeline and Theresa. There I was, stuck in traffic beside her. I avoided making eye contact. I pretended I hadn't seen her. I couldn't handle a confrontation at that moment. But I could see her out of the corner of my eye, waving her hands wildly, trying to get my attention.

Why was she trying to harass me? Why did she enjoy terrorizing us? What was her conflict with me? Why did she crave conflict? It was so exhausting for me, but somehow energizing for her. She knew she scared us and she loved that, if she loved anything.

My brother was gone. My Dad was now gone as well. I was trapped near this belligerent woman, suspected of involvement in my brother's death, while she acted like an animal trying to instigate God-knows-what.

Katrina had refused to allow my parents to go to the kids' grandparent's day at school before Dad passed away. Then she forbade Lindsey and Sawyer from attending their grandfather's funeral—now this.

This was a breaking point, all the accumulated provocations piled up. I lost myself. I forgot fear and was no longer afraid. I was barred from moving forward by traffic. There was no available flight. This game had to end; I didn't want to play.

I yanked my car out of traffic and pulled into the Farm Bureau parking lot. Before I could get out of my car, Katrina ran over and ripped my door open so that it bounced on the hinges and almost closed again on the rebound.

"What is your problem?" I asked, still sitting in my car. I wanted to know why she couldn't leave me alone. None of this made sense to me.

She didn't say anything. Her stare was cracked by her signature smirk, peeling over her teeth. She laughed, and then slammed my door so hard that it rocked my car.

The whole show had been for the sake of watching me scramble. Her ego was in constant need of confirmation. She wanted to remind herself that I was scared of her.

The cocktail of emotions I had been prudently attempting to file away and process, piece by piece, now overwhelmed and hijacked me. I was not myself. There was no thought, only emotion.

A surge of adrenaline shot through me. In one motion I hopped out of my car and walked after her. She turned around and saw me coming; she walked faster, shifting gears from a self-congratulatory victory stroll to a quicker step. I could tell she was trying not to walk too fast, not wanting to appear like I had surprised her.

Katrina leapt the last few steps to get back to her truck before I reached her, but she still had her window down from antagonizing me a minute earlier. She started her truck, hurrying to roll up the power window, but before she got it all the way up, I reached through, grabbed her hair and pulled it down so that her chin pointed up.

"I don't know what your problem is! I don't know why you're doing this!" I yelled. "I know you did something to David and you're being investigated!"

I punctuated this statement by slamming her head down on her steering wheel which made a loud thud and honked her horn. That sound snapped me out of it. I have never been aggressive before or after that. I don't know where the strength came from. The fight response had taken over after so many flights hadn't provided any security from this woman who hunted conflict.

Suddenly realizing what I had just done, I turned away and walked toward my car.

"Hey," Katrina yelled after me.

I turned.

"I'm going to make you an anti-freeze cookbook."

I had no idea what that meant. I wasn't inclined to decode whatever clever insult this was. In my fluster, I could not process this cryptic joke. For now, I was content with having finally stood up to her. I didn't say anything and walked away as she laughed. With my back turned, I noticed her laughter had the same cadence as crying.

As I collected myself on the drive home, I began to question what Katrina had been doing at the Farm Bureau insurance office. The investigators found that she had several large bank deposits that amounted to a sum much larger than what David had in life insurance coverage. Unfortunately, we weren't able to find out where these deposits came from except for one which was a policy from J.C. Penney, which I doubt David knew anything about. I wondered what other insurance policies David hadn't known about. A Farm Bureau policy could have been one of those large deposits of unknown origin.

A moving truck was seen at Katrina's house a few hours later. She was running. She was taking Lindsey and Sawyer with her.

Katrina's laugh had been taunting, like she knew what she was doing by threatening me. She was leaving a clue. She is intelligent in a manipulative sense, cunning but reckless. Her cryptic cookbook comment betrayed her unabashed arrogance. She was flying high, too close to the sun. Her wings of deception were melting like a wax mask.

I was young and Katrina obviously didn't feel the need to worry about me. This over confidence was her Achilles heel. She must have felt invulnerable to make that suspicious comment. An innocent person wouldn't risk arousing an accusation, a self-preserving guilty conscience wouldn't self-incriminate so coolly for the sake of cheap emotional gamesmanship. Whatever she had done, she was proud of it. She wanted us to know what she had done and she wanted us to watch her get away with it. She wanted us to feel powerless. This was part of the game. This was her caustic humor.

Katrina could be quick witted. Early on I had enjoyed her company because she was funny, but I came to realize her humor was cutting and abusive. She was only funny until you were her target. She would bait people into laughing along with her, and then watch them realize the joke was on them. She felt no shame in proclaiming her intellectual superiority in passive-aggressive heckles. No opportunity was wasted to make someone feel smaller. I still question if she is as intelligent as she would like us to believe or, if instead, she desperately needs others to believe that she is superior. I wonder if her bully narcissism is dependent on that validation.

Initially, I regretted telling Katrina that she was under investigation, because it had caused her to run. Still, her immediate flight from the state was incriminating in itself. I wished she had stayed in town while we built up our case against her. Maybe she would have made more mistakes. I expected she would continue to provide evidence of her instability regardless of where she lived.

Our investigators were aware my parents had already filed for grandparent's rights after Katrina had refused to allow them to see Sawyer following David's death. By leaving Arkansas, Katrina was in contempt of court. Our investigators and attorney hoped to use this as an opportunity to bring her and the kids back to Arkansas where she might divulge more clues and incriminate herself or lead us to more evidence.

Investigators traced Katrina through her state-hopping run for several years. She ran through Wyoming, Utah, California and many other states along the way, but she never stayed long enough for investigators to get close and serve a subpoena.

I missed Sawyer. As I laid in bed into the night, waiting for elusive sleep, I wondered how he was fairing being drug around the country by his volatile mother. I imagined him being enrolled and withdrawn from a series of schools full of unfamiliar faces.

Sawyer's resemblance to David was striking. Was that resemblance haunting Katrina? This possibility only made me worry more. It could be dangerous for him to remind his mother of David. What might Katrina do now that she was alone with Lindsey and Sawyer? What might she do without David to fend her off and provide sanctuary? As Katrina ran, she was without her typical predations of family and friends. She would have to create new targets to satisfy her. Sawyer and Lindsey would be even more vulnerable to her paranoid flights of fury.

Years passed with no answers despite our certainty that Katrina was at least partially responsible for David's death—either through negligent homicide or premeditated murder. It didn't make sense that a former police dispatcher was unable to call an ambulance or seek help directly behind her house at the Sheriff's Office. It didn't make sense that she had somehow evaded an autopsy. It didn't make sense that she had falsified paperwork and that the hospital payment records had mysteriously disappeared from their files. It didn't make sense that this chronic instigator fled the state after hearing she was under investigation.

Increasingly, I thought Katrina's mention remarkable that her mother lost her first husband unexpectedly at a young age, just like David. I thought of the mystery surrounding Lindsey's unknown father. I remembered what the psychiatrist had said about learned behavior. Was this a pattern?

I tried to find an address, a phone number, but all I could dig up was an email address, Katrina007@... I hadn't been interested in those movies but I recognized the reference. It was just like Katrina to give herself a secret agent email address, but beneath her juvenile fantasy it seemed taunting now as well. I would keep that email address for years, unsure of how it could be useful.

I began to fear Katrina was getting what she wanted, that she was winning by teasing us with just enough evidence to realize she had done something, but not enough to convict her so that now we had to watch her get away. This open wound couldn't heal. The emotional scab continually itched and fell off and periodically we bled anew.

We were afraid that we would never see
Lindsey and Sawyer again. We wouldn't.

Chapter 12

Impossibly, two years had already passed since David's death. Katrina continued her flighty tour of America with Sawyer and Lindsey in tow.

Finally, we felt we had reached a turning point when we heard that State Police had agreed to meet with us. Mom and I bundled all of our file folders of notes and statements and relevant legal data. We knew that State Police would see evidence of foul play, cause for further investigation. State Police would be on our side after this and I hoped Mom could start saving the money she had been spending on private investigators.

But our meeting didn't go as expected. We met with one detective. He seemed bored with us. He asked my Mom some questions—dates and times—but he wasn't interested in the falsified paperwork or the cancelled autopsy or any of the many conspicuous details recorded in our bulging files. He mostly nodded. He wasn't interested in the big picture, only dates and times. It was a short exchange. He told us that he would let us know if anything changed and shuffled us along.

Mom was crestfallen but upon seeing the look of defeat in my face, she straightened her back and assured me that this was only a temporary setback. Right was still on our side. The law was still on our side. We had to keep trying, for David, and for his children.

Over the next several years we sent hundreds of letters requesting clearance to exhume David's body and have an autopsy performed by a medical examiner so that we could fully investigate the circumstances of his improbable death. We made every appeal we could, hoping to be granted an autopsy that should have already occurred, according to State Law. Our team of investigators and attorneys continued to build a case but we all knew that the autopsy was the key to a conclusion.

Our persistent appeals to politicians and the judiciary of Arkansas were met with ineffective back-patting, if we were answered at all. I cringe at the thought of how many letters from family members, friends, and attorneys went unread altogether.

Whenever we were blessed with a response from any of these public servants it was always an evasive, noncommittal message couched between the form letter introduction and form letter conclusion. The signatures were all stamped. I tried to imagine the people employed to answer letters on behalf of these officials. How many identical letters were sent out each day?

My mother was summarily advised to let it go, to keep calm and carry on. She was condescendingly reminded that she was only one of many grieving mothers requesting "special" attention to their case. This opposition was disorienting. We were referred through a variety of offices and on to a variety of departments and back again in looping, recursive evasions. We were a buck to be passed. Several leaders were out of the office so often that we began to wonder if their phones were ringing in forgotten PO boxes somewhere. We hadn't realized that access to the law was a special request.

Each of these state officials, including the State Prosecutor, who has now served in another public office, refused to lend a hand. Evidently, our case wasn't politically expedient enough to garner any consideration. This negligent and slothful public service led me to believe I had been naïve to expect otherwise. This apathy reminded me of Katrina's indifference to Madeline's request for one of David's old hats.

As we reviewed these mounting stacks of refusals, a conspicuous similarity glared off the pages of gaudy, gold-leaf letter head. They had each already been consulted by the Perry County Sheriff's Department (PCSD) and understand there is no need to proceed with an autopsy."

This was unbelievable, yet undeniable. Our investigation was being sabotaged by the very public office charged with protecting us and serving justice. Someone within the Sheriff's Department was working against us. It was terrifying. It was like being robbed by the police department then asking to speak to the chief, only to have him tell you that he had already been informed by the officers that there was not a problem. The only available conduit to higher offices was the barrier; who could we appeal to now?

Mom and I considered contacting the FBI but doubted our case would receive much attention since our own State Police were disinterested. We thought we could work our way up the system. I did not understand why the PCSD was the gatekeeper to our state's leaders. David hadn't even been pronounced dead until he arrived at St. Vincent in Morrilton, which is in Conway County—so why did Perry County Sherriff's Department have such a decisive influence on the matter?

Without political weight, or a fortune to bankroll an endless investigation, our effort was beginning to feel futile. Knowing that the Sheriff happened to be Cain Perry's best friend was salt in our sore. As City Marshall, Cain could act on behalf of the elected Sheriff whenever he was unavailable, or even just for the Sheriff's convenience.

I thought of Katrina's relationship with Cain, and Cain's proximity at the Sheriff's Office to David and Katrina's house. Children could play a game of catch between those two addresses. The PCSD was close enough that if Katrina had screamed for help she surely would have been heard, yet she hadn't thought to scream or run next door on that night when David's health rapidly deteriorated. Perhaps she didn't want to implicate herself in her affair with Cain by running over for help. It isn't impossible to imagine Katrina being motivated by such selfish reasoning, but everyone already knew about her and Cain's affair. There was no secret to keep; in fact, I'm confident she *wanted* everyone to know. This dramatic irony was part of her performance, a strategy to score points in her vindictive game. If she had been preserving her reputation by avoiding going to Cain at the Sheriff's office for help, why would she allow Cain to walk over around eight p.m. earlier that evening when a neighbor saw him at David and Katrina's house? Surely, having your lover come over to your husband's house isn't the most subtle way to arrange a rendezvous. David would be dead only hours after that sighting. Coincidences aren't usually as neatly woven as this.

I remembered that my sister Sarah had tried to call David that night around 8:30, only half an hour after Cain was seen there. Katrina told Sarah that David was too sick to come to the phone. He would be dead around 10:30, if not earlier. God knows what David endured during that window of time. I remembered how my brother's hands had become stuck, cupped, frozen in their grasping. The funeral director had found that strange.

It remains incredibly frustrating to see unsuspicious deaths routinely served with an autopsy. This is necessary to rule out any unknown factors. Meanwhile, we face this uphill battle for an autopsy that would shed light on the mysterious death of a healthy young man.

There was nothing standard about my brother's sudden death, not even procedure, and non-standard procedure is ripe for misfeasance. The cause of death could have even been a matter of public health. A healthy young man emitting dark fluid suddenly passes and it is deemed a heart attack; what if he had contracted some viral contagion? The Arkansas

Department of Health would need that information to issue an alert in order to protect citizens.

After years of waiting for permission to exhume David's body, years of being denied an autopsy, and closure, I finally decided I had to leave this town. Here, I was accosted at every corner with reminders of tragedy. I was saturated in the grief-preserving brine of the place. This half-life felt purgatorial. My parents had deeded me land here and those acres made me feel connected to my dad but I didn't know how I could ever build a life in this place.

All of the unexpected resistance to our investigation had burdened me with a jaded fatigue. My spirit was squelched. My future was delayed, deferred, pending. My desires had become rust-bound, weathered in the corrosive salty damp of persistent sweat and periodic tears. A deep dull soul-bruise throbbed along with my pulse.

If I didn't make a decision to divert my path, I feared I might get stuck in this dark cloud forever; not just in Perryville, but in that space of time between the loss of my brother and father. Headlines and pop culture from that time are embedded with associations for me. To this day, a few pop songs from the 1990s have the vertiginous power to transport me out of an elevator, or department store, or restaurant and back to that blue-filter place and slow time.

Perryville had become suffocating. I had to escape this cultural claustrophobia. I was flanked by loss and amnesiac justice. Home had become an overwhelming *memento mori*, a reminder of death. I knew I could not bloom in this place. I asked myself, *what would David do?*

He would look for an opportunity to change this course. He would make a decision. He would move forward. He would give himself permission to take intelligent risks. He would set his mind to a goal. He would work hard so that even if he failed, he would have the peace of knowing the failure was not his, that it was part of a larger plan that was beyond his control. And having done his best work, he could be content that he did not know. I decided I had nothing to lose by venturing out into the world for a positive change.

It was now four years after David's death. I just finished college and was reflecting on my life before this trauma, searching for a direction to take. I missed modeling and acting. It was something I had been involved in as a child and through high school. I had always told people I wanted to someday own a talent agency. That goal fueled me through innumerable photo shoots and acting auditions. But after I lost David and my Dad, that aspiration faded. Maybe now was the time. I decided to train deeper in the acting world. I was reinvigorated by the challenge of it. I felt strong. This was a strange route to arrive at this new confidence. Emboldened by the certainty that all my worst fears had already come true, I could easily numb myself to the fear of rejection. What was rejection after losing two relatives and being evaded and ignored by the state legal structure?

I wanted this goal to work toward. The more I could learn the more I could someday teach other aspiring actors and models. I wanted the healthy diversion. It was refreshing to dedicate myself to the task, especially to something I loved so much. Unfortunately, the possibility of competing against hundreds of other actors and models, seemed like a more realistic and attainable goal than justice for David at this time.

I travelled all over to compete in the long audition process, and to my jarring surprise, I made the cut many times! It felt like a win for me as well as for Mom. I was so excited each time to have good news to share with her. This ray of sunlight helped me grow. In this environment I could allow myself to trust people again. Finally, I had found positive experiences. In the midst of such incredible new opportunities, a bitter sweetness occurred to me. I might never have followed my childhood dream had it not been for the tragedy that pushed me from home.

I dedicated myself to the arts, modeling my own work on the work ethic I had seen in David. I began to understand how hard work was therapeutic to him in times of stress or conflict. My demanding schedule allowed no time to dwell on anything else. After years away, I returned to Arkansas.

As soon as I came back to Perryville, I was confronted by all that I had run from. The dark cloud had waited patiently for me to return to its shadow. There were triggers everywhere. It hurt to drive by

David's old house and see the Sheriff's Office directly behind it. I drove by the rental property that David had saved so diligently to purchase and then remodeled himself. This was the investment property that Katrina pawned off at bottom dollar for quick cash a week after his death. It had fallen into a dilapidated state that David would have never allowed. Lose shingles shivered in the breeze. The damp from a morning rain seemed to be the only adhesive keeping many of them attached. The house had lost all of the pride he had built into it with his hands.

The sight of a restaurant where David and I often ate together puddled my eyes with the memory of silly conversation, sibling banter that could never recur. You assume that what you'll remember most are the weddings, the birthday parties, the graduations and vacations, but I was increasingly struck by reflections of meals and Sunday afternoons that we don't often take pictures of, those mundane conversations on drives that we don't think to record. They are the gems mined of memory.

I remained restless. After doing some research on a internationally renowned private investigator and his Dallas-based firm, I travelled to Texas to enroll in private investigating courses taught by him.

I found him to be one of the most interesting people I have ever met. He had the aura of an authentic secret agent. He was bright-eyed, sharply intelligent, incredibly deductive, and extremely Texan. His investigative specialties were murder, kidnapping and extortion. He had authored several books about his work on high-profile cases.

I wanted to learn the lingo and study the various avenues available for accessing information. I hoped that this innovative curriculum, along with his lectures, would equip me to pursue more answers about what happened to my brother. Our struggle with law enforcement and the justice system had burned away my naïve assumption that I could count on experts to inform me. There were no reliable narrators.

I knew I had to do something. But I didn't know what there was to do. I needed to study to find out. If I didn't, who would? Your case is never as important to law enforcement as it is to you. My mother was exhausted; my siblings didn't talk about it anymore. They didn't talk to each other much these days, either. David's death had brought everyone together for a time, but my Dad's death did the opposite. There was no obvious plan of action. There was no clear end in sight.

Although I learned a great deal in these studies, I came to realize that the curriculum on the subject assumed a more functional system. After considerable research I reached a point where it was not my understanding that was insubstantial but this system I was trying to navigate. The standard protocol which so much of this top-shelf advice was predicated upon had either been largely ignored by the crime lab and state officials or the procedures were intentionally sabotaged as Katrina and Cain tried to cover tracks.

It was less clear how exactly Cain was involved, but his name kept coming up. Katrina's efforts to throw us off her trail were obvious in her flagrant falsification of paperwork. The very fact that she was trying to obscure something assured me that there was something worth looking for, something Katrina wanted to hide. What else might she have tampered with? These gray areas surrounding the remaining questions in our investigation were not covered in my textbooks.

There were no shortcuts, no exhaustive references to consult, no proven step-by-step guides. Instead, the truth of how any investigator pieces together a story from fragments and threads and dead ends was hidden in those spaces between lines of text, in the margins, tucked in spaces small enough to get lost in. This case wasn't being handled by the book so the books held limited explanations. It would take persistent trial and error, research, endurance, and a clear mind to take on this tangled task.

My greatest discovery during this time was uncovering a few more insurance plans that Katrina had taken out but we still don't know exactly how much money Katrina received or who paid for David's E.R. expenses. During my training Katrina's old email address, Katrina007, resurfaced as I revisited the stacks of letters, statements, insurance documents, notes and research that had accumulated. One of the investigator's associates noticed the email address and gave me a funny look. He recalled that the Bond movie that had come out most recently when Katrina would have made that email address was *"License to Kill."*

I vaguely remembered hearing that title. It came out in theaters shortly after that curious incident with the SWAT team. I read about the film, hungry for any minor lead to chase. I had to keep moving forward. This installment of the Bond series differed from the others in the franchise with its portrayal of a darker version of Bond who resigns his position and goes rogue for revenge but, of course, comes out the hero in the end. It was easy to imagine Katrina attaching herself to this embattled narrative. This email address was yet another example of Katrina's pathetic narcissism but proved little else.

The more I learned the more I thought of all the questions that could be answered with a belated autopsy. After all I had learned, the fact sadly remained that there could be no autopsy without Katrina's approval because she was still legally next-of-kin. According to lawyers and other investigators the only way to get an autopsy was to prove suspicion. But what more could be done? How many more suspicious details would I have to find before it was enough?

This entire experience had made me cynical of our legal system and sure that it was either inept or corrupt; I found no comfort in either possibility. I found this legal hierarchy, charged with enforcing laws, serving justice, and seeking truth, to be a dry husk—all shiny badges, glossy business cards, waxed patrol cars, and gilded echo-chamber offices—all glaring and impervious props.

It was dizzying to lose my faith in this system of social order and security at such a young age. The law is not solid; it is selectively permeable. It bars and allows things discriminately. Money and good ole boy networks lubricate and wield the law or disarm and declaw it, whichever suits the ulterior agenda at hand or accommodates the lazy indifference of the day.

My research confirmed what I was afraid I already knew. We were right; the law was on our side, but the law was not enough. The autopsy should not have been something we had to fight for—State Law required it. Where do you go when the law is not enough? I had reached a wall.

During a conversation after a training lecture, I was asked what had brought me there, so I shared my reason for enrolling in the courses. I explained coincidence after coincidence regarding the circumstances surrounding David's mysterious death. The investigator nodded keenly as I recounted our efforts to find paperwork that had conspicuously disappeared and explained the peculiar influence the Perry County Sherriff's Department had in the case. He was supportive and told me that he looked forward to witnessing the conclusion of our case. It was incredibly validating to hear this from such an exemplary investigator.

Meanwhile, the very bureaucracy designed to keep these things from happening, and to repair them when they do, offered no assistance, and worse, was thwarting those willing to seek out the muddy truth. The system was sepulchral, providing only the appeasing illusion of equal treatment under the law. I had to acknowledge at an early age that money and resources are directly correlated to your experience within the state justice system. Public servants ignored us like wait staff we hadn't tipped.

With enough money, it appeared that any verdict under the sun could be ruled, while more humble cases were ignored. We were told that various offices' caseloads were too large for them to deal with us anytime soon. We were told that other offices were still reviewing the details of the case. We were told that some officials had already spoken with PCSD and wouldn't be talking to us about it. Innumerable calls and letters were never returned at all. Without clearance to exhume David's body, the medical examiner would be unable to perform an autopsy. Without the autopsy we couldn't answer our biggest question.

I wondered how many times this had happened to families just like ours who never made the news. How many other lonely family struggles had been refrigerated by disinterest until they became cold cases? I have undeniable proof that something this crazy can happen to anybody, since it happened to us. This cannot be easily excused as something that *used* to happen long ago in a more primitive time. This didn't happen one-hundred years ago, it was the 1990s.

When the justice system fails you, you want the perpetrator to at least feel burdened by human guilt. It is small consolation, but it helps preserve a healthy sense of retribution in the world. But I can't take any comfort in such a fantasy. I doubt Katrina is haunted by any recurring demons tormenting her from within. This is the deepest injustice—that she likely feels good about herself.

Perhaps she is as adept at deceiving herself as she is at deceiving others. After convincing herself that none of it happened, this is yet another "win." She can feel righteous, even victimized. Having imbibed her own illusions, her deception continues. In this way she can add self-awareness to the list of shallow relationships she maintains for exploitation. Her social circle is a toolbox full of people to use, including her own children.

Katrina had begun telling Sawyer that Madeline wasn't his sister immediately after David's death, but thanks to Facebook, Madeline was able to contact Sawyer. Her long-lost little brother was in his twenties now, they were both adults. She hoped they could meet each other after all these years. Instead, he sent an offensive response expressing his disinterest in meeting her. But I can't blame him; who knows what he has been told.

Sawyer's sweet face, so strongly favoring David, is frozen in time. In my mind, he is still a sweet six-year-old boy, pedaling around our neighborhood on that bike my parents bought him. In my mind, Sawyer never

misses an opportunity to watch Teenage Ninja Turtles
or Power Rangers.

Chapter 13

With the legal system failing us, I opened my mind to nontraditional investigation. I had to find a way to keep moving forward even if our investigation was losing steam. The search for an answer to my brother's death could not end with this whimper.

I learned of famous psychic, Carol Pate, on the television program *Psychic Detectives*. I discovered that she was located in Little Rock. I was intrigued by her work and began reading about the numerous occasions she had assisted law enforcement in Arkansas and surrounding states. She has been featured in several major television productions including: *The Geraldo Rivera Show, Unsolved Mysteries*, and *Larry King Live*. Personally, I was put at ease by her Christian foundation; she's a minister in addition to her consulting work. I was amazed to learn that she had been assisting with investigations since her childhood.

Although I had never envisioned myself consulting a psychic, I decided I had nothing to lose by hearing what Carol Pate had to say about our case. I had to do something—anything—to keep moving forward. I wanted to test her against my skepticism.

I made an appointment for a consultation with her without providing my name. One of the associates at her office informed me that I should bring a sample of handwriting or photos related to whatever I wanted to speak with her about. My earnest need to avoid stagnancy had driven me to this unlikely appointment.

When I arrived at the address, I found her office to be a renovated house. Inside, the atmosphere was relaxed and intimate, a comfortable contrast to the glossy chambers of attorneys and judges. One of her associates led me into a room to meet her.

"Do you have any questions or pictures?" Ms. Pate began.

"I do have some pictures. Please tell me what you can about these people," I said. I didn't tell her my name.

The two pictures I had brought along were of Katrina and David. I donned my best poker face and told her nothing about the photos or myself. I didn't want to reveal any detail that she could use to fabricate something. I gave no information regarding these people, not my relation to them, or my suspicions. Objectivity was my goal.

I was comforted when she began by thanking God for her gift. She then took both photos between her palms in her steepled hands, like she was praying. She closed her eyes. We sat in silence. The quiet poured in around me until my ears rang at a tinnitus pitch. I grew uncomfortable. Was it silly of me to have come here?

She opened her eyes a moment, then took only the photo of David in her hands and closed her eyes again. I sat, debating whether I should have come, staring at her clenched eyes.

They flashed open.

"I don't know if you know this...I'm not sure I should be the one to tell you if you don't already know this...I don't want to upset you, but this man was murdered."

It was a relief to hear someone finally state the ugly truth, but I maintained my stoicism. I wanted her to keep talking without my apparent relief or anxious questions influencing what direction this consultation took. I didn't concede a shred of information.

Ms. Pate quickly closed her eyes again, and after a few moments, said, "Anti-freeze...in his food and drink."

At the mention of that word, my memory shot directly to that confrontation with Katrina sixteen years earlier in Perryville. For almost two decades that cryptic phrase had taunted me. Days went by with that threatening clue continually replacing itself in my mind. For years I had alternately pushed the thought away and analyzed it, trying to determine if it was just another instance of her incendiary nature or a concession betrayed in the heat of that moment. Now I understood.

"...Sweet tea," Carol continued. "Did this man drink a lot of sweet tea?"

My mind's eye flashed back to that day, within a week of David's death, when I had stayed with the kids. They were thirsty but they refused the sweet tea. Katrina had strictly forbidden it because it was "Daddy's tea."

I remained tight-lipped as I tried to process what this meant. These revelations raised so many new questions. There was some relief in having what I'd always known acknowledged by Ms. Pate. David's death was not a natural accident. My brother's relationship with Katrina had begun and ended with a drink.

Ms. Pate picked up the other picture, Katrina's picture, and held it between her palms. After a few seconds, her brows knitted tightly, as if bearing some invisible burden.

"This is a very cold person," she said finally. A tremor ran through her, very subtly, but visibly, like she had been chilled by a gust of cold air from an open door. She put the picture down quickly and took a deep breath. "This woman was involved in the death of that man," she said, gesturing toward the picture of my brother. "But someone helped her," she continued, "an accomplice, someone in law enforcement. This person is frustrating an investigation. Her accomplice is tall and very skinny."

I thought of Cain Perry, tall and bone-thin, acting on behalf of the Sherriff as City Marshall.

"You should know, she will do this again," Carol added softly as I tried to absorb all of this.

"If I bring you a picture of another individual, can you tell me about them?" I asked.

She agreed, so as I left I began constructing a plan to get a picture of Cain. He was now retired from law enforcement and operated a pitiful used car lot showcasing eight late-model automobiles. They were over-waxed to a superficial gleam, the tires heavily sprayed with gloss to obscure their dry-rot cracks.

Cain had many serendipitous connections to this case. He had been intimately involved with Katrina. He had been seen at David's house hours before his death. He was the right-hand-man to the Sherriff, whose office had blocked all requests for an autopsy that should have been guaranteed by State Law without contest.

Katrina had vowed to my shocked aunts that she would "get David back." What kind of coincidence was it that she had chosen to seek out a revenge affair with a man of Cain's particular influence, even though he was much older than her? Because of his familiarity with the process of investigations, Cain would have known exactly how to thwart one. It could be as simple as misplacing paperwork, as simple as dropping letters in the trash, or failing to relay a message. And if a busy judge or politician didn't follow up, it was over, another dead-end.

As the City Marshall, vested with the power to act as Sheriff, he would have had many opportunities to sabotage correspondences or other aspects of the investigation. He could have easily disguised his meddling as assistance, as if he was doing the Sheriff a favor by handling paper work.

I thought again of the neighbor's sighting of Cain at eight o'clock at David's house and of the window of time between Sarah's unsuccessful call for David at 8:30 and Katrina's call to my father at 10:30.

David was a strong man. Katrina was small. Perhaps she had utilized her tall friend Cain to overpower David. Katrina could not have done that alone. I thought again of David's hands, petrified in that strange grip.

My mind spun, connecting new pieces of this puzzle. A bigger picture was coming together. But I wondered, what was Cain's motive? Did she promise him part of the insurance money? We still don't know how much she got. There were several insurance policies she claimed, some from David's previous employers. I doubt David knew anything about these other policies.

What strings of Cain's did Katrina pull in order to draft him as her tool? Maybe she fabricated a story to give Cain a rationalizing hook. Maybe she claimed that David was abusive or told Cain some other lie to mobilize him and rationalize her scheme. It might have been as simple as threatening to inform Cain's wife of their affair. Maybe she charmed him into it. I am sure she made the vainglorious and venal Cain Perry feel very big and strong, like the hero who must step outside of the law in order to deliver a perversion of justice, a trope carried out in so many police dramas.

After Katrina had involved Cain however she had, he would never be able to walk away. He could never give her up without incriminating himself. I suppose that was a calculated part of her plan all along. She is arrogant, but she is not stupid. She knew that once she got his hands dirty he could never wash his hands of this. This engineered safeguard would not only encourage Cain's silence, but also his continued protection of her. If law enforcement found her they would likely get to him as well. Cain would have to protect Katrina to protect himself. She hooked an indentured guardian with useful influence through this paternal romance.

Their affair had never made sense to me before. I was not surprised that she was unfaithful so much as I was surprised by whom she chose to be unfaithful with. Katrina's insecurities about retaining her handsome husband were transparent in her jealous maneuverings, yet she sought an affair with Cain Perry, a much older man, who despite considering himself very attractive was not widely thought to be.

Katrina and Cain did have their similarities, though, and when I considered them, along with all Katrina had to gain by manipulating Cain, the affair made sense. They were both cheating on their spouses. But while it was obvious that she wanted David to find out, I doubt Cain knew that was part of the game. Cain had a wife he didn't want to find out. They were both immune to criticism. Neither of them thought it possible to hold too high an opinion of them. They mutually reinforced and enabled each other's narcissism.

Katrina would have had the upper hand, of course. She would have gained Cain's favor through flattery, by stoking his ego to burn for her. She would have alternated this approach with a manufactured dependence, allowing Cain to feel like he was the boss, oblivious to the fact that he was following tracks laid out before him. These shows of dependence would have given her access to the influence of his office and he would have believed he was acting of his own volition, as if it was his idea.

Katrina found Cain malleable, gullible, and eager to please her. She validated his rose-colored self-image. He had a deference reserved for Katrina alone. She could make him feel like he had known her forever. But she knew him better than he knew.

I considered how all of our attorney's letters had been forwarded to the Perry County Sheriff's Office. Perhaps the reason we kept getting so close to Katrina then losing her as she hopped across state lines was because she was being tipped off by someone within the Sheriff's Office.

The use of anti-freeze, an automotive fluid, seemed like something that a male might suggest, especially one as familiar with cars as Cain. He would know how Katrina, being next of kin, could finagle a way to evade an autopsy despite State Law. Cain would have known how to thwart the law with his bravado and influence as City Marshal.

Soon after my meeting with Ms. Pate, I stopped off the highway at Cain Perry's trailer office and walked around the grassy gravel lot. I chose a vehicle and walked a few circles around it, peering in windows, pretending to be interested. I knew he was watching through the blinds of his cramped little office, purveying his stamp-sized kingdom.

Before long I heard the creak and yawn of his screen door and he sidled over to make a deal, still walking as he always had with his waist dragging the rest of him along. His boots slid forward a little after each step, pebbles skittering from his shuffle as he approached.

Cain had aged roughly. He looked like a different person. His eyes were still narrow, like he was perpetually peering through blinds, even out here in the light of day. Maybe it was too bright for him outside, beyond his shadow. He was paunchy and soft, whereas the Cain that used to strut around town when I was in high school was always tugging on his gaudy belt buckles. He was always rocking on his heels, swaggering with his hips jutting forward. He had been skeletal, with bushy sideburns. Cain had worn an attitude of superiority on the sleeves of his pressed uniform, and around the full-brim Sheriff's hat that he peered narrowly out from beneath. Maybe his eyes remained squinted because of the dependence he had developed for that stripe of shadow cast by his hat.

This weathered Cain, however, was far from his previous strut. A cigar no longer protruded cockily from his jaw. His teeth were yellowed and narrow. His once sharp triangular nose now drooped at the end over his mustache. I wondered if his demons had done this to him.

He didn't recognize me. I might not have recognized him if it weren't for the business card he handed me. It had been nearly twenty years since I had last seen him. I asked some questions about the vehicle: mileage, year, if the AC stayed cold in summer. I told him I needed to take some pictures so my brother could look at it. I pulled out my camera and began snapping pictures as I circled the car, trying to catch Cain in the frame, but he kept stepping out of the picture. After a few laps around the vehicle I finally got a picture of him.

He moved to shake my hand, but I lost my nerve. I could not bring myself to shake this man's hand, so I fidgeted with my camera strap and pretended to drop my keys, thanked him and left.

I returned to Carol Pate's office with the new picture. I had hardly sat down when she saw the photo in my hand.

"I'll take a look," she said, "but I really don't have to. I already know."

Chapter 14

I had been inspired to consult Carol Pate out of desperation and had been quite skeptical, but her insight into our case held too many critical details to be ignored. The validation and direction our meeting provided refueled my will to move forward. The questions our conversation raised offered hope and reminded me there was more that I could do. I had to find some detour around the systemic stonewalling of our investigation.

I began researching the effects and symptoms of anti-freeze poisoning. During the 1990s, anti-freeze poisoning was one of the most common methods of matricide, or spousal murder, in the United States. This rash was partially the result of the high-exposure media frenzy surrounding sensationalized anti-freeze poisonings, such as the murders committed by Jennifer Castor and Lynn Turner. Because of the ensuing copycat effect, many states implemented new laws requiring the inclusion of bitter additives in anti-freeze to change its naturally sweet taste. Both intentional and accidental poisonings occur every year.

Due to its sweet taste, pets and other animals often lick up puddles of leaked anti-freeze in parking lots and driveways. This toxic sweetness could be easily masked in sweet tea. I recalled, with a cringe, a conversation I had heard at a farmer's co-op between two men discussing anti-freeze as the best means to keep pests out of their barns.

David would eat anything. If something didn't taste right, he wasn't the type to make a comment about it. He was sweet-natured. Katrina's volatile nature filled even short exchanges with kindling for argument. Any comment on her cooking or sweet tea would've sparked a fire of rage or downpour of self-pity. David chose his battles more carefully than that.

This was yet another way Katrina had exploited his sweetness. He enjoyed whatever was served to him. He would never have complained about her cooking, even if he had noticed an inexplicable sweetness. He would never mention that there was something a little off about the tea, even if it tasted syrupy, or had a peculiar plastic twang. David was polite, possibly to a fault.

I learned that it takes only three ounces of ingested anti-freeze for it to be fatal. These lethal three ounces don't have to be consumed all at once. With gradual consumption of poisoned tea, only a little at a time, the masked sweetness never arousing suspicion, the compound's byproducts built up to a terminal toxicity.

Ethylene glycolis the chemical commonly known as anti-freeze. When ethylene glycol is ingested it oxidizes into glycolic acid, and then into oxalic acid. As the body tries to breakdown the chemical, the nervous system, heart and kidneys are all damaged as crystals of calcium oxalate form in body tissues.

David had been poisoned slowly, insidiously. This was not a crime of passion. Crimes of passion are usually violent, impulsive and poorly planned. This was cold animal dominance, without heat. This scheme required an architect. It was premeditated. It took her several days to carry out this murder, longer to plan it. She had no fear of losing her will to kill in the middle of this calculated process. I wondered how many times David had politely thanked her when she offered to cook dinner, or handed him a cold glass of sweet tea.

It was painful to learn that even a large dose of ethylene glycol can be remedied with timely treatment. But help was not sought by that former police dispatcher, even with the Sheriff's Office, a former EMT, and the paramedic's station all within the same block of her home.

The similarities between symptoms of anti-freeze poisoning and the symptoms that David exhibited just before he died are too similar to be explained away as happenstance. The fluid he emitted from his nose and mouth, which I already knew wasn't characteristic of heart failure, came up in repeated accounts of anti-freeze poisoning.

Katrina had been content to accept David's mysterious death as an act of God, but there were human fingerprints on this tragedy—imperfections, sloppy fraudulence, and arrogant threats. Perhaps Katrina had come to believe that she was the God presiding over this human drama.

I reflected back on Lindsey's concern that day, years before, that David had been yellow and had kept getting up to look at himself in the mirror. This was only a few days before we lost him. I knew now that David was jaundiced. His body was struggling to combat the toxin. Even though Lindsey was a little girl, she knew something wasn't right. The man she had always known as her Daddy had a sallow complexion, an early sign of kidney failure.

I remembered my worried brother-in-law Thomas telling me how David's legs kept falling asleep during their fishing trip. Thomas told me that within the week of David's death. The poison must have begun crystallizing by that point. Ethylene glycol causes heavy circulatory blockage, the type of clotting that required the funeral director to use a three-point injection to embalm David's body.

Ethylene glycol is an alcohol. It is a derivative of the same alcohol people drink for pleasure, but it inebriates in a deadly way. That intoxicating side-effect explained David's dizzy spells leading up to his death. David never missed work, but he stayed home the day he died. I still chide myself for not going over to check on him after I saw him drive to the corner store. Maybe I could have convinced him to go to the doctor. He was always so stubborn about going for his checkups.

I thought of that window of time beginning with the sighting of Cain at David and Katrina's house around 8:00 pm, then Sarah's call at 8:30. Katrina told Sarah that David was too sick to come to the phone. Only two hours later, just after 10:30 pm, when Katrina knew my mother would have already left for work, Katrina called not the police or ambulance next door to her property, but our elderly father. It was Dad who ultimately called the ambulance, after realizing several minutes after he arrived that Katrina had not done so already.

What had Katrina done in those hours between 8:00 or 8:30 and 10:30 that night? Did Katrina call Cain to assist in restraining my brother? David was a large man and Katrina was small. If David had tried to get up from bed, or leave the house, or go to the phone for help earlier in the evening, before he got too weak, he could have easily overpowered Katrina. But he would have become exponentially weaker as his body struggled to break down the poison. I'm sure he resisted as long as he was able, before her cowardly venom immobilized him. I thought of his hands, a sign of his strength, gripping life.

There had been a pitcher of cold sweet poison in the refrigerator, "Daddy's tea." How did she dispose of what poisoned tea remained? What did she do with that pitcher? I wondered if she washed it. I wondered if she had been casually washing all of David's poisoned cups and putting them back in the cabinets for her children to drink from. Did she wash dishes that night while David suffered in the next room? Did she kill time waiting for the poisoning to become irremediable? Did she watch the clock until 10:30 when she knew Mom would be gone and Dad would be home alone? Did she throw the pitcher and cup away? Did she task Cain with disposing of them? Did she dutifully take the trash out before anyone else arrived, casting away the evidence?

Like her chosen poison, Katrina was easily

masked. Her most destructive weapon, which enabled all of her toxic engineering, was a capacity to conceal her emptiness. She was a heat haze mirage, a shifting surface, a gaseous indifference that could take any form useful to her. She was a glossy shell, refractive like the manicured nails she habitually clicked together and picked at.

Anti-freeze is a dangerous chemical in any quantity and there are laws regarding its safe disposal. I doubt Katrina took such precautions. Did she flush it down the toilet or pour it down the sink? Did her brew seep into water sources over years, killing plants, fish, pets, and animals wherever it dripped? How far did her poison travel before it diluted?

Even less than 1% solution of ethylene glycol kills plants. I remembered that patch of bald lawn that I had seen near Katrina's porch as I walked up the stairs the day after the funeral. I remembered seeing a dead cat in the corner of her yard. Maybe it had not been hit by a car after all. Perhaps that dark fluid puddled around its mouth was the same fluid that David had emitted in the ambulance. Perhaps that cat had lapped up a sweet dampness by the porch.

Once again, I felt my effort to prove suspicion had reached a wall. All of these suspicious details weren't enough to gain clearance for exhumation. I could not call this place my home any longer.

When I got to a strongpoint about six years ago I decided to return to sell the land my father had left me. Holding on to it for so long made me feel as if I could hold on to him. But I now knew that I needed to leave that place behind. The bad memories had grown to overwhelm all the good ones. I know my father understands.

Since I sold the land, I have only returned periodically to place fresh flowers where David rests outside of Perryville. I returned this past year to replace the flowers.

I wondered what might have changed in that small patch of Arkansas where our family was changed so much. When I initially moved here as a child, decades ago, it was surrounded by hardwood forest. The Ouachita National Forest includes half of Perry County. But now most of those surrounding hardwoods that fanned reds and yellows and oranges from the ridgelines in autumn have been replaced by commercial pine, grown to supply pulp to the paper mill by the Arkansas River.

I drove past all those unfolding rows of soybeans, past the cluttered yards off the highway, across the gorgeous land of Perry County. Rolling over those hills, I could feel the latent flow of the land rippling beneath me. I travelled the winding highways between patches of green sewn with barbed wire fences and forestry service roads and sutures of red clay. Crop dusters stuttered and coughed overhead. They flew alarmingly low, suspended in the sky like the cascades of colorful chemicals they dust over the fields.

I looked for signs of change in town. A few restaurants had closed. A few restaurants had opened.

A new gas station had opened across the street from the old gas station, which still advertised a cheap gas price from another time. The grocery store had burned. Perryville still lacked a traffic light, I noticed. It is still too small for that kind of regulation.

When I reached our old neighborhood a torrent of emotions washed over me. So many feelings mixed together. Anger was tempered with sadness. Nostalgia was tempered with regret that I hadn't somehow found a way to prevent all of this turmoil. Holographic memories from twenty years earlier projected themselves onto these quiet, grass-choked streets. Sawyer rode his bike in broad circles yelling for his Daddy to watch. Madeline and Lindsey played house by a tree in the yard and took turns bringing entrees of sticks and pinecones and dandelions to David where he sat on the step watching them play.

This sylvan scene evaporated as I got close enough to see the Sherriff's Office and the ambulance directly behind the property. Help had been so close.

None of the life in that daydream was still here. These places are empty lots now, home only to gray slabs, and wind-combed grass. There was nothing here for me.

I arrived at David's resting place to refresh the flowers and a have a moment there to remember him, to pray for guidance and reflect and talk to him. I stared across the cemetery grounds under a wide blue sky, and imagined our family and friends here so many years before, harboring suspicions but still too overwhelmed with mourning to chase all the coincidences. The cemetery gates still held my mother's maiden name. It had been her family's plot for many generations before Perryville was established. Her family eventually donated it to the city.

Suddenly I had the sensation of being watched. I felt that curious weight of other eyes. I turned to look behind me and my eyes were drawn to a curious headstone, tall and black. Something drew me to it. In all my visits to this same spot I had never noticed it but when I read it I understand why I had been pulled there.

It read:

"Dearly beloved avenge not yourselves but rather give place unto wrath for it is written Vengeance is mine I will repay saith the Lord
Romans 13:19

HOMICIDE,
Perry County Sheriff's Department"

I came to find out this epitaph was written at the behest of a mother who lost both of her sons in separate instances to the guns of the PCSD. Each instance was full of hearsay, and rife with delayed notification of other authorities by the attending officer. In one case that single officer was Cain, in another it was Cain's son. The facts about each case are muddy at best, intentionally murky, no doubt, but it was widely known that there were persistent personal grudges between those brothers and Cain and his son. In both cases, it was an officer's word against a citizen's. Any interest in further investigating these cases was quickly squelched.

I could relate to that kind of stonewalling. I could relate to being squelched by the gatekeepers. Despite the PCSD's continued claim that there is no need to allow an autopsy, I hope you can see I have a clear purpose. My goal in sharing this story of heartbreaking deception is to reveal that this case does not have to remain cold.

Due to the nature of anti-freeze poisoning it is still detectable to forensic pathologists, even decades later, because it crystallizes in the bone. This is the next step forward to a belated conclusion to this thwarted investigation. How can they deny us that? Arkansas State Law has been ignored and declared optional by an office whose duty it is to uphold the rule of law.

David's body is stored in an oxygen-sealed vault and is perfectly preserved, but when the body comes in contact with oxygen, it will disintegrate. However, thanks to advancements in forensic pathology, medical examiners can now open caskets in oxygen-free tents so that tissue is not destroyed. An autopsy is more than possible, it is necessary. The longer we are ignored, the easier it is for new officials and new judges to ignore us. The buck passing gains momentum as years pass. There are financial limitations to our appeals. We cannot afford to continually lobby for equal access to the law.

Katrina has become comfortable again, in the same way she once became comfortable in her pregnancy lie after getting married and having moved. She has become comfortable enough to come out of hiding in the last few years. She is now a first-grade teacher in Oklahoma, despite having told us, that day at my aunt's house, that she doesn't like kids.

It terrifies me that she has found a way to weasel into the trusted role of being a teacher. It terrifies me that she has finagled her way into this readymade mask. It is obvious why she would be attracted to the authority of that occupation. She can claim a certain amount of integrity by association, in the same way she gained some people's trust by her relation to David and his candor. Like a cold-blooded animal, she gains proximal warmth from the people around her. I imagine her lording over a classroom of young children, in total control, always her word against theirs. An elementary environment is the perfect court for her playground games.

On her classroom web page I discovered she was voted Teacher of the Year for 2008-2009. What an incredible performance. In a picture of Katrina holding her plaque, I see that her costume has changed. She has traded her false blonde for a red-orange only found in crayon boxes and hair-treatment bottles. Her dark roots still show and form a widow's peak. According to her award profile, "she has taught both 1st and 2nd grades." She was "born in Kansas. She has lived in Texas, Colorado, Wyoming, Arkansas, and of course

Oklahoma." This list of states is spouted as if she had gone on some enlightening, character-rounding tour of America, rather than running from police and investigators to avoid a contempt of court charge.

I read on. She "was married to a wonderful man named David from 1984 to 1997 when he passed away suddenly." I could not believe she had included this in her award profile. This had clearly been written by Katrina, about herself. I recognized her aggrandizing voice in the language. This statement about David was interesting for a variety of reasons. She claimed that she was married to David from "1984 to 1997," yet they were not married until 1987. David was a junior in high school in 1984. At first, I assumed that this was just a sloppy oversight, but no, I knew better than that. It was obvious Katrina had written this blurb about herself; she was too calculating for this to be a simple mistake.

Her profile went on to mention that "she has two children," Sawyer and Lindsey (Madeline was not included, unsurprisingly). Then it hit me, the false marriage date was for Lindsey. Katrina had always told Lindsey that David was her father. But for the math to work with Lindsey's birthday, Katrina and David would need to have been married since 1984. This lie was decades in the making; Katrina couldn't let it dissolve with a public award profile. Lindsey would surely see it.

It was strange, I felt, for her to include her marriage to David at all. Her cloyingly idyllic description is entirely disconnected from the reality. Decades after his death, she now finds him to be a "wonderful" man, and feels inclined to mention that he died "suddenly." This was to cultivate pity and create intrigue, another way to pollinate conversations without people asking her questions.

Katrina goes on, continuing to paint this picture, telling everyone that "she cares for her mother...whom [sic] lives with her now." Furthermore, "she believes the greatest gift of teaching is that no matter what, the students always love her, even when they are in the upper grades." She is overcompensating. I have never heard as self-centric a motivation for teaching as that. There is something rotten beneath the overripe sweetness.

Madeline is now a grown woman. She lives in Oklahoma and she has a friend with a daughter who was in Katrina's class. Katrina made a point of telling the little girl, who told her Mom, who told Madeline, how much she loved her husband David. Why would she say that to a first-grader decades after her husband had passed? Because she knew it would travel back. She was aware of the tenuous connection between this little girl and Madeline. Katrina's game continues. Deferred justice has emboldened her.

I knew that Madeline had found Sawyer on Facebook so I was curious if I might find Katrina's profile on the social network as well. How was she presenting herself to the world now? What face was she wearing? I knew it would be different from the face I saw accepting a Teacher of the Year award. She was only comfortable in fluctuation. Her hair was now blonde, bangs teased to fluff.

The "About Me" section of her profile was as overwrought as her award profile. But in this opportunity to write about herself, her favorite subject, her vengeful nature bled through the veneer.

"My life has been good, but not easy. I love being a mother, aunt, sister, friend and teacher. My true friends know who they are, just as those I don't care for, know who they are. Never have been good at hiding my feelings about anything. Never have been able to perfect the poker face. Pretty open and often, much too quick to speak, about my feelings in all areas. Have a tendency to be very critical of myself, and to be honest, of others as well. I'm still a work in progress, as it should be. Sometimes I find myself moving backward, struggling to get back on the forward moving waves. For those I love, I love with all my heart, soul, and energy. For those that don't matter, well, they just don't matter. Live for today as it may be your last. Life is too short, so have as many loves, laughs, and adventures as you can. I've lost my husband, one child, my parents, and came close to losing myself. I intend to live this life the best way I know how, and teach as many along the way as possible."

Had any of her students' parents read this? Her grammar alone might worry a parent before they had even gone on to discover her appetite for vengeance and drama and self-pity.

191

From her own self-description we know that she does not make a secret of who she does not care for. That temperament can't be conducive to a healthy and equitable learning environment. My eyebrows rise at her self-deprecating "never have been able to perfect the poker face." If only she had saved that hard stone face for a benign poker game rather than her game. She is honest enough to tell us that she is often critical of others. While she is proudly relentless in her judgment of others and does not let people doubt whether she likes them or not, she allows herself the right to be a "work in progress."

Careful that we don't miss how forgiving and loving she is, she reminds us that "For those who don't matter, well, they just don't matter." Her advice "to live for today as it may be your last" reads more like a threat than a cliché, coming from her.

Her penultimate line struck me, not for its false lament for David, but for the mention of a lost child. I wondered if she was still referencing the fictitious miscarriage that had been disproved decades earlier. I imagined her recycling that story in each of her newly penetrated social circles, juicing it for all the pity she could wrench from the tale, each rerun a more practiced performance.

But I was mistaken. Her mention of a lost child was not referring to that delusory miscarriage, but to her daughter Lindsey, her favorite. Lindsey was now married and had a child of her own. Evidently, Lindsey is still very much alive, but has no interest in speaking to her mother. I wondered which of Katrina's many dishonesties and manipulations had finally pushed Lindsey away. Did Lindsey discover that life-long lie about who her father was, or was it something else?

I imagine Cain and Katrina are still in contact in order to continue their corroboration. In a way, Cain will be handcuffed to his temptress forever. To protect himself, he must always protect her. Cain's son went on to become Sheriff of Perry County. He is the first Perry County Sheriff in history to be elected by write-in, which I find suspicious. I worry that this new cog in their self-lubricating machine will continue to frustrate our effort for an autopsy.

Katrina had Cain Perry's help, but she also benefitted from the inaction of masses. She is indebted to the many individuals who cleared her path and covered her tracks, both intentionally and negligently. I fear what people can be ignorantly capable of doing. I wonder how many people kept their suspicions to themselves for fear of becoming one of Katrina's targets, or for fear of losing credibility for sharing outlandish but true observations of her volatility.

In a murder trial she might get off with an insanity plea. I have no doubt she's intelligent enough to convince people she's medically mad. She wouldn't have to contrive proof of that. She firmly believes, maybe correctly, that she is intellectually superior. Katrina is confident that she can afford such taunting indulgences as her "anti-freeze cookbook" comment.

She believes she is too smart to be apprehended by our law-enforcement structure. So far, she's right.

I have made my peace with the fact that she will find retribution in this world or the next and it is not my responsibility to make that judgment. No degree of shallow vengeance has potential to undo any of our struggles; no amount of her pain could relieve our past or present or future suffering. But above all else, David's children need to know the truth. Lindsey deserves to know. His son, Sawyer, deserves to know. I am sure he has been made to think badly of his father, if he has been told anything at all.

I always felt like I had to do something, that I had to find something to do, but what was available after facing so many closed doors for so long? How could I move forward? I am not an attorney, or a politician, or a power-broker, or a Sherriff. At first, I didn't think the path forward would be a book, but I found a voice and I need to tell this story as much as it needs to be heard.

His life was stolen. His justice has been postponed. Although the scar will always remain, it is time for this wound to close. An autopsy is the missing piece. It is the next step in reclaiming our missing peace.

This story doesn't have to end here.

Made in the USA
San Bernardino, CA
14 October 2013